EXPANDING
Global Military Capacity
for Humanitarian Intervention

EXPANDING
Global Military Capacity
for Humanitarian Intervention

Michael E. O'Hanlon

BROOKINGS INSTITUTION PRESS
Washington, D.C.

Copyright © 2003
THE BROOKINGS INSTITUTION
1775 Massachusetts Avenue, N.W., Washington, D.C. 20036
www.brookings.edu

Library of Congress Cataloging-in-Publication data
O'Hanlon, Michael E.
Expanding global military capacity for humanitarian intervention /
Michael E. O'Hanlon.
    p.   cm.
Includes bibliographical references and index.
    ISBN 0-8157-6442-1 (cloth : alk. paper) —
    ISBN 0-8157-6441-3 (pbk. : alk. paper)
1. Peacekeeping forces.   2. Humanitarian intervention.   I. Title.

JZ6368 .O36 2003
341.5'84—dc21   2002151828

9 8 7 6 5 4 3 2 1

The paper used in this publication meets minimum requirements of the
American National Standard for Information Sciences—Permanence of
Paper for Printed Library Materials: ANSI Z39.48-1992.

Typeset in Sabon

Composition by R. Lynn Rivenbark
Macon, Georgia

Printed by R. R. Donnelley
Harrisonburg, Virginia

To the people of Kikwit
and to my fellow
former Peace Corps volunteers
in Congo/Zaire

CONTENTS

CONTENTS

Tables

Figures

FOREWORD

Despite a number of helpful interventions designed to save lives in recent years, the international community has fallen short in its overall response to ethnic and civil conflict since the end of the cold war. Far from becoming an "age of peace," as the first President Bush deemed it, the era has been characterized largely by ongoing and brutal wars in places ranging from Rwanda to Chechnya, from the Balkans to Somalia, from Sri Lanka to Sierra Leone. Since September 2001 concern about civil conflict has been largely supplanted by the war against terrorism. But that very war has also served to underscore the importance of addressing civil conflict, given how al-Qaida has benefited from the safe havens and resources it could find in conflict zones such as Afghanistan, Somalia, Yemen, and Liberia.

Stopping civil war is far from easy, and the standard for success should not be set too high. That said, the international community does have powerful interests, both moral and strategic, in trying to quell the world's most lethal conflicts, as well as those wars that leave large swaths of the developing world mired in chaos and underdevelopment. And in the past decade, it has often failed to do enough to put an end to this type of war. Sometimes the problem has been the sheer difficulty of devising a workable strategy for stopping a given war, sometimes the problem has been the fact that policymakers have been involved in addressing other problems that consumed most of their time and attention. But at other times, it has been the lack of deployable and effective military forces that has been the major barrier to action. Especially in situations where the United States was not willing or able to lead a rapid intervention, the international community has often been stymied in its ability even to consider a serious response.

In this short study, Michael O'Hanlon addresses this problem. He surveys the state of global military capabilities and assesses how far short they fall relative to the actual need for intervention forces capable of saving lives in humanitarian and peace operations. He then proposes a blueprint for how countries ranging from Europe to Africa to East Asia can improve their capacities for rapid, forceful interventions without increasing defense budgets substantially. Among his important recommendations are that western military aid and assistance programs for African countries be expanded substantially, and that countries such as Japan reconsider their traditional reluctance to engage in multilateral military missions that may require the active use of combat power to quell conflict and save lives.

STROBE TALBOTT
President

Washington, D.C.
November 2002

ACKNOWLEDGMENTS

My thanks to the U.S. Institute of Peace for financial support; Richard Haass and James Steinberg for guidance with the project; Micah Zenko and Aaron Moburg-Jones for research assistance; James Schear and Steve Kosiak for reviewing the manuscript; and numerous officials in the U.S. government for their time and assistance.

EXPANDING
Global Military Capacity
for Humanitarian Intervention

CHAPTER ONE

SAVING LIVES WITH FORCE

Since the end of the cold war, a number of writers and pundits have forecast increasing conflict and violence around the world. Largely because of the Balkan wars and the 1994 Rwanda genocide, they have predicted escalating ethnic conflicts, a global contagion of substate violence, and a coming international anarchy in the less-developed parts of the world. By their logic, the end of superpower conflict lifted a restraint on numerous countries and ethnic groups that had previously limited the prevalence and severity of warfare. These observers also thought the negative side of globalization—rising expectations and widening gaps between rich and poor, set against a backdrop of growing populations and deteriorating environments—would exacerbate tensions and produce the kindling for civil conflict in many regions.[1]

1. See Robert D. Kaplan, *The Coming Anarchy: Shattering the Dreams of the Post Cold War World* (Random House, 2000);

Thankfully, however, the worst of these fears has not come to pass—at least to date. Civil warfare has not escalated appreciably since the latter part of the cold war, and in fact some data sets show that it has declined somewhat in recent years.[2] UN peace operations did expand greatly in number at the end of the cold war.[3] In addition, large-scale conflict did occur in Europe for the first time since the end of World War II. Those facts do not mean, however, that the prevalence of civil war increased or that wars became more severe.

Nonetheless, the international community faces a real problem and a major challenge. Civil conflicts remain numerous and deadly. Trends in demographics, economics, the global weapons market, and international politics suggest that, whether or not

Thomas F. Homer-Dixon, "On the Threshold: Environmental Changes as Causes of Acute Conflict," *International Security*, vol. 16 (Fall 1991), pp. 76–116; Norman Myers, "Environment and Security," *Foreign Policy*, no. 74 (Spring 1989), pp. 23–41; George D. Moffett, *Critical Masses: The Global Population Challenge* (Viking, 1994); Jessica Tuchman Mathews, "Redefining Security," *Foreign Affairs*, vol. 68 (Spring 1989), pp. 162–77; John D. Steinbruner, *Principles of Global Security* (Brookings, 2000), pp. 139–46; Boutros Boutros-Ghali, *An Agenda for Peace, 1995*, 2d ed. (New York: United Nations, 1995), p. 7; and Daniel Patrick Moynihan, *Pandaemonium: Ethnicity in International Politics* (Oxford, England: Oxford University Press, 1993).

2. See Yahya Sadowski, *The Myth of Global Chaos* (Brookings, 1998), pp. 130–40; Ted Robert Gurr, Monty G. Marshall, and Deepa Khosla, *Peace and Conflict 2001* (College Park, Md.: Center for International Development and Conflict Management, 2001), pp. 7–9; and Peter Wallensteen and Margareta Sollenberg, "Armed Conflict 1989–99," *Journal of Peace Research*, vol. 37, no. 5 (2000), p. 638.

3. See William J. Durch, "Introduction," in William J. Durch, ed., *The Evolution of U.N. Peacekeeping* (St. Martin's, 1993), pp. 7–11.

these conflicts get worse over time, they are unlikely to diminish much further on their own.[4] Several hundred thousand people still lose their lives each year due to the direct effects of war and to war-related famine and disease. Very serious and deadly conflicts continue in Algeria, Burundi, Congo, Sudan, Colombia, Palestine and Israel, Indonesia, and Kashmir. Dozens of smaller conflicts are under way elsewhere, in places ranging from Nepal to Chechnya to Georgia to Somalia.

These wars seem unlikely to lead to large-scale armed conflict among the world's major powers, but they have many other serious costs. They have an obvious and extremely tragic toll in lost human lives—with most of the dead being innocent noncombatants and a distressingly high number of combatants being child soldiers.[5] They can produce conditions that provide terrorist groups with havens or sources of illicit income, as in Afghanistan, Somalia, and Sierra Leone in recent times, as well as with motivating causes, as in much of the Middle East. They do much to keep Africa mired in misery, economic stagnation, and disease. They can cause massive refugee movements, which have the potential to affect the domestic stability of nearby countries. They also undercut the common western argument that democracies protect and promote human rights.

4. Carnegie Commission on Preventing Deadly Conflict, *Preventing Deadly Conflict: Final Report* (New York: Carnegie Corporation, 1997), pp. 11–22; and National Intelligence Council, *Global Trends 2015: A Dialogue about the Future with Nongovernment Experts* (Washington, D.C.: Central Intelligence Agency, December 2000), pp. 7–9.

5. There may be 200,000 child soldiers in Africa alone; see Ministry of Defence, United Kingdom, "The Causes of Conflict in Africa," London, 2000, available at www.mod.uk/index.php3?page=2526, part I, p. 6.

The frequent failure of the industrial democracies to do much about such conflicts weakens their moral authority and their international legitimacy as global leaders.

The world community cannot excuse its neglect of many civil conflicts on the grounds that humanitarian intervention would violate international law and the UN Charter. Russia and China are only occasionally inclined to wield their UN Security Council vetoes against such operations. NATO's war against Serbia over Kosovo, which proceeded at first on a shaky international legal foundation, underscored that difficult cases can arise. For the world's most deadly conflicts, however, legal mechanisms for intervention are generally available.[6] Individuals from developing countries themselves now argue that sovereignty requires a sense of responsibility on the part of national leadership toward its citizenry; to ignore that responsibility is to surrender many of the traditional prerogatives and protections of state sovereignty.[7] A number of developing countries are also willing to use national military assets to forcibly reduce the severity of civil conflict within their own regions.[8] For example, the Constitutive Act of the new African Union,

6. See Catherine Guicherd, "International Law and the War in Kosovo," *Survival*, vol. 41, no. 2 (Summer 1999), pp. 19–34.

7. See Francis M. Deng and Terrence Lyons, eds., *African Reckoning: A Quest for Good Governance* (Brookings, 1998); and Francis M. Deng and others, *Sovereignty as Responsibility: Conflict Management in Africa* (Brookings, 1996).

8. See, for example, the comments by various African military officers as summarized in Ericka A. Albaugh, "Preventing Conflict in Africa: Possibilities of Peace Enforcement," in Robert I. Rotberg, ed., *Peacekeeping and Peace Enforcement in Africa: Methods of Conflict Prevention* (Brookings, 2000), pp. 111–210; see also Adekeye Adebajo and Chris Landsberg, "The Heirs of Nkrumah: Africa's New Interven-

which replaced the Organization of African Unity in 2002, notes in Article 4 "the right of the Union to intervene in a Member State pursuant to a decision of the Assembly in respect of grave circumstances, namely: war crimes, genocide and crimes against humanity."[9]

To be fair, governments and international institutions have made numerous efforts to mitigate civil conflicts since the cold war ended. Longstanding peacekeeping missions continue in places such as Cyprus and the Sinai. In addition, a new and more comprehensive type of approach—involving not only peacekeeping but also election monitoring, demilitarization, and state building—has been applied in places such as Cambodia, Mozambique, Haiti, El Salvador, and the Balkans. Several of these missions have been successes, or at least partial successes, in the sense that intervention made conditions better than they might otherwise have been. Specifically, missions in Cambodia, Mozambique, Albania, Kosovo, and East Timor all probably made a significant difference for the better. The NATO-led mission in Bosnia ultimately helped matters as well, even if the roles played by NATO and UNPROFOR in the first three years of the war were less impressive.[10] Even the aborted mission in Somalia mitigated the famine there, saving tens of thousands of lives.

---

tionists," *Pugwash Occasional Papers*, vol. 2, no. 1 (January 2001), pp. 72–86.

9. See Organization of African Unity, "Constitutive Act of the African Union," Lome, Togo, June 12, 2000, available at www. sudmer. com/cen-sad.

10. See William J. Durch, "Keeping the Peace: Politics and Lessons of the 1990s," in William J. Durch, ed., *U.N. Peacekeeping, American Policy, and the Uncivil Wars of the 1990s* (St. Martin's, 1996), pp. 1–34.

Missions in Angola and Rwanda were outright and major failures, however, in the sense that bloodshed intensified after the deployment of foreign forces. Moreover, the world's noninterventions in places such as Sudan and Liberia allowed extremely brutal wars to continue even though it seems likely that effective missions could have been designed to stop or to contain them.

On balance, the international community deserves no more than a mixed grade for its humanitarian military operations of the first post–cold war decade. It has made reasonable efforts, though not always with excellent results, in places where humanitarian imperatives have been juxtaposed with strategic interests—the Balkans, Haiti, Afghanistan. It has been much less inclined to act decisively elsewhere. Surveying his native continent of Africa in 1998, for example, UN secretary general Kofi Annan put it bluntly and accurately: "By not averting these colossal human tragedies, African leaders have failed the peoples of Africa; the international community has failed them; the United Nations has failed them."[11]

Throughout this period, much of the international scholarly and diplomatic community has sought better means of dealing with severe civil conflicts and their human consequences. Insights have been gained about the strong linkages between economic crises and violence, the need for early action when possible, the role of war crimes processes, and the importance—but also the difficulties—of crafting exit strategies.

11. Kofi Annan, *The Causes of Conflict and the Promotion of Durable Peace and Sustainable Development in Africa*, April 21, 1998, quoted in Donald Rothchild, "The U.S. Foreign Policy Trajectory on Africa," *SAIS Review*, vol. 21, no. 1 (Winter/Spring 2001), p. 202.

However, much of the literature on peace and conflict resolution suffers from several excessively optimistic assumptions that require rethinking. Some of the optimism concerns the potential for negotiations to prevent or stop conflict; some of it relates to the military feasibility of forcibly quelling warfare when negotiations fail. Taken together, this literature tends to underrate the importance of physical intervention capabilities for saving lives with force if other means fail.

For example, proponents of peace operations and preventive action often assert that neutral and relatively apolitical deployments can solve many civil wars by "separating militias" and "disarming combatants." Sometimes such missions will work. In many cases, however, militias and combatants will not wish to be separated or disarmed—and would not assent to such operations if asked. In other words, warring parties are frequently motivated by more than fear of the other side; they often choose war to pursue power, wealth, or land.[12]

Many argue that if only better preventive action were undertaken by the international community, many wars could be avoided or nipped in the bud.[13] That is a good argument in favor of greater international support for development assistance, debt relief, favorable trade agreements with developing countries, and favorable prices for drugs to counter HIV/AIDS; it is a good argument for preventive negotiations and crisis diplomacy as

12. See Richard K. Betts, "The Delusion of Impartial Intervention," *Foreign Affairs*, vol. 73, no. 6 (November/December 1994); and Stephen John Stedman, "Alchemy for a New World Order," *Foreign Affairs*, vol. 74, no. 3 (May/June 1995).

13. See Carnegie Commission on Preventing Deadly Conflict, *Preventing Deadly Conflict*.

well. However, preventive action will not work in places where the chance for it has already been missed and conflict has begun.[14] In addition, the list of places where preventive action might be required is quite long; policymakers will not always be able to send forces where they might be helpful, and they will sometimes guess wrong about where they are truly needed.[15] Prevention will often fail.

Others claim that just a small standing UN force could make a major difference in reducing civil conflict around the world. Proponents often cite a goal of 5,000 troops, motivated in large part by the claim of Canadian general Romeo Dallaire that such a capability, if added to his small UN force in Rwanda in 1994, could have stopped the genocide there.[16] However, Rwanda is a small country that is not representative of many places where civil conflict occurs. In addition, although there is little doubt that General Dallaire would have used 5,000 more troops bravely and with some effectiveness, it appears a low estimate

14. On the promise and the limits of mediation, see I. William Zartman, ed., *Elusive Peace: Negotiating an End to Civil Wars* (Brookings, 1995).

15. Arnold Kanter, "Memorandum to the President from the 'National Security Advisor,'" in Alton Frye, ed., *Humanitarian Intervention: Crafting a Workable Doctrine* (New York: Council on Foreign Relations, 2000), p. 9.

16. See Carnegie Commission on Preventing Deadly Conflict, *Preventing Deadly Conflict*, pp. 59–67; Linda Melvern, "Genocide behind the Thin Blue Line," *Security Dialogue*, vol. 28 (September 1997); Scott R. Feil, *Preventing Genocide: How the Early Use of Force Might Have Succeeded in Rwanda* (New York: Carnegie Corporation, 1998); for more documentation of this line of thinking, see Alan J. Kuperman, *The Limits of Humanitarian Intervention: Genocide in Rwanda* (Brookings, 2001), pp. 84–87.

even for Rwanda, based on standard criteria for sizing intervention forces.[17] Furthermore, if there were two or more simultaneous conflicts requiring rapid attention, such a force would certainly be much too small, necessitating tragic choices about whom to help.

The international community needs to organize itself more systematically to deal with the problem of civil conflict. The military capacity of the great powers for humanitarian or peace operations is probably adequate for conflicts in which their strategic interests are also clearly at stake. However, the international community has insufficient capacity for addressing other conflicts. Such capacity is only a prerequisite to successful intervention, not a sufficient condition, but it is a prerequisite that is often lacking.

Rather than thinking in terms of a 5,000-person UN force, the international community should develop the capacity to deploy and sustain much larger numbers of troops abroad,

17. There are various ways of estimating force requirements using generic, standardized, rules of thumb. Some link necessary forces to the size of opposing forces and suggest that outside troops be at least as numerous as the largest indigenous army or militia. Others tie requirements to the size of the civilian population base needing protection and assume that 2 to 10 troops are generally needed for every 1,000 inhabitants of a troubled region or country. By the first metric, an intervening force in Rwanda might not have had to exceed 5,000 in strength, since that was the size of the Rwandan military at the time (not counting irregular forces). By the second, however, at least 15,000 troops would have been needed to protect a population of 8,000,000. See James T. Quinlivan, "Force Requirements in Stability Operations," *Parameters*, vol. 25, no. 4 (Winter 1995–1996), pp. 59–69; and Michael O'Hanlon, *Saving Lives with Force: Military Criteria for Humanitarian Intervention* (Brookings, 1997), pp. 38–42.

above and beyond those forces it possesses today.[18] The international community should try to double its current intervention capacity. That is, it should develop the wherewithal to deploy and sustain about 100,000 more troops than it can today. It should create substantial capabilities because serious conflicts, even if generally not numerous, can each require tens of thousands of troops if they are to be handled properly. Smaller numbers of elite or even private soldiers can sometimes handle discrete tasks, but the broader problem of stabilizing a country requires significant forces.[19] Once a decision on intervention is reached, moreover, it is generally preferable to send forces promptly and in decisive quantities. Such an approach conveys resolve, discourages resistance, and improves the odds of success—especially in the most difficult of conflicts.[20] It also offers the greatest hope of ending a con-

18. For another argument in favor of building up the capacities of states, rather than international organizations, for humanitarian interventions, see S. Neil MacFarlane and Thomas Weiss, "Political Interest and Humanitarian Action," *Security Studies*, vol. 10, no. 1 (Autumn 2000), p. 115.

19. For a good discussion of some of the potential, but also the limits, of private security forces in civil conflicts, see Greg Mills and John Stremlau, eds., *The Privatisation of Security in Africa* (Johannesburg, South Africa: South African Institute of International Affairs, 1999).

20. See Richard N. Haass, *Intervention: The Use of American Military Force in the Post–Cold War World*, rev. ed. (Brookings, 1999), pp. 87–94; see also, Annika S. Hansen, "Lines in the Sand: The Limits and Boundaries of Peace Support Operations," in Mark Malan, ed., *Boundaries of Peace Support Operations: The African Dimension*, ISS Monograph no. 44 (Pretoria, South Africa: Institute for Security Studies, 2000), p. 23.

Characteristics that make conflicts particularly difficult to terminate include the involvement of multiple parties with access to

flict with minimum loss of life to intervening soldiers as well as local populations.[21]

Standing up a dedicated UN force with 100,000 or more personnel would be very expensive and politically challenging. Fortunately, it is not necessary. National armies around the world are already paid and equipped, so building on their capacities rather than creating new institutions from scratch is the soundest course of action.

Even if individual countries provide the bulk of the forces, there is a need for standing multilateral capabilities in certain realms. Greater numbers of talented people and greater financial resources are needed for UN command and control capabilities, for example.[22] Other organizations, including NATO, various subregional groups in Africa, and others, also need to improve their command, control, and planning capabilities for humanitarian intervention and peace operations.[23] In many cases, such regional or subregional organizations will be better choices for

---

resources and arms and with fundamentally divergent aims. See Lakhdar Brahimi and others, *Report of the Panel on United Nations Peace Operations* (New York: United Nations, 2000), pp. 4, 9.

21. See Michael Walzer, *Just and Unjust Wars* (Basic Books, 1977); Andrew S. Natsios, *U.S. Foreign Policy and the Four Horsemen of the Apocalypse: Humanitarian Relief in Complex Emergencies* (Westport, Conn.: Praeger, 1997), pp. 119–20.

22. See Holly J. Burkhalter, "Memorandum to the President from the 'Secretary of State,'" in Frye, *Humanitarian Intervention*, p. 32; United Nations Association of the United States of America, *The Preparedness Gap: Making Peace Operations Work in the 21st Century* (New York: United Nations Association of the United States of America, 2001), pp. 38–41.

23. Daniel Byman and others, *Strengthening the Partnership: Improving Military Coordination with Relief Agencies and Allies in Humanitarian Operations* (Santa Monica, Calif.: RAND Corporation,

leading humanitarian or peace operations than the United Nations, especially when operations are complex and forcible.[24] Regarding physical capacity for intervention—the primary focus of this study—the case is strong that it should rely primarily on states, however.

Even if the international community expands its intervention capabilities dramatically, it should often choose not to intervene in civil conflicts. This point is elaborated in chapter 2. In many cases, the prospects for success do not justify the associated costs and risks. However, decisions about whether to intervene should be based on the merits of a given case—on detailed considera-tion of a conflict at hand. They should not be predetermined by the fact that the international community simply lacks the nec-essary military capabilities to make an intervention practical. In today's world, that is often precisely what occurs.

There are limits to what robust and timely military interven-tions can accomplish, even in situations where the international

---

2000), pp. xiii–xxi; and Eric G. Berman and Katie E. Sams, *Peace-keeping in Africa: Capabilities and Culpabilities* (Geneva, Switzerland: United Nations Institute for Disarmament Research, 2000), pp. 278–79.

24. See, for example, Lori Fisler Damrosch, ed., *Enforcing Restraint: Collective Intervention in Internal Conflicts* (New York: Council on Foreign Relations, 1993); Michael Hirsh, "Calling All Regio-Cops," *Foreign Affairs*, vol. 79, no. 6 (November/December 2000), pp. 2–8; and Edward C. Luck, "Good Cops, Bad Cops?" *Foreign Affairs*, vol. 80, no. 2 (March/April 2000), pp. 194–95.

Work is also needed in other realms. For example, the U.S. govern-ment does not do a consistently good job of coordinating humanitar-ian relief to displaced populations. See, for example, Department of State, *Interagency Review of U.S. Government Humanitarian and Transition Programs* (Washington, D.C., 2000), available at www. gwu.edu/~nsarchiv/nsaebb/nsaebb30/index.html.

community does decide to respond. For example, in the case of the Rwanda genocide, so much killing happened so quickly that even a U.S.-led operation to stop it could have taken several weeks to complete its deployment and hence might not have saved many of the victims.[25] However, in many cases, rapid and assertive intervention can succeed in quelling conflict, provided that policymakers are prepared to act on compelling evidence when it is presented to them.[26] Even in Rwanda, the robust and prompt deployment of force could have made a major difference. Before the genocide began, a robust preventive force could have been effective. After the genocide began, the very act of beginning a deployment might have affected the behavior of the locals and persuaded them to desist or to scatter out of fear of retribution. Even if a preventive deployment had not been tried, intervention after the genocide began could have saved 200,000 or more victims. This calculation is based on the conservative

25. An important work on this subject is Kuperman, *The Limits of Humanitarian Intervention*. Kuperman appears somewhat too pessimistic about the number of air deployment corridors and regional airfields that intervening forces could have used had they attempted to be creative and maximized the urgency of their response. For example, aircraft could have flown not only down from Europe but over from the Pacific or Latin America, and could have used numerous regional airfields instead of just one or two. In that event, substantial forces might have arrived by early May, and 300,000 deaths might have been averted (even without assuming that the international community's commitment to respond would have had any effect on the rate of killing in April). But Kuperman's overall message about the difficulties of rapid response is still persuasive.

26. For a history of how they have often not done so, see Samantha Power, *A Problem from Hell* (Basic Books, 2002).

assumption that an intervening force could have arrived by mid-May if a decision to intervene had occurred by mid- to late April and on conservative assumptions about how quickly a force could have been airlifted into Rwanda.[27]

Moreover, given the extreme pace of the genocide, Rwanda was very much the exception and not the rule, so the international community should hardly be discouraged by this one example. In recent wars that have also been characterized by enormous (and, in some cases, even greater) death tolls, such as those in Somalia, Sudan, Angola, and Congo, the unfolding of the tragedy has been far more gradual.

This study lays out an agenda for increasing the international community's military capacity to stop deadly conflict through peacekeeping, peace enforcement, or forcible humanitarian intervention operations. It estimates how many troops and police might be needed if the international community took a more comprehensive and rigorous approach to stopping warfare in cases where civil conflict was severe and the prospects for restoring peace were reasonably good. It then suggests a plan for sharing among key countries and regions the military burden of quelling conflict. Its primary purpose is not to suggest how U.S. forces could handle such missions more easily and frequently, given the existing and unique demands on American armed forces around the world. It does offer modest sugges-

27. Alison L. Des Forges, "Alas, We Knew," *Foreign Affairs*, vol. 79, no. 3 (May/June 2000), pp. 141–42. For an analysis that may be somewhat too optimistic about the capacity of the international community to stop the genocide early, but that is nonetheless valuable as a counterweight to Kuperman, see also Feil, *Preventing Genocide*.

tions for changes in American military posture, but it focuses at least as intensely on how countries in western Europe, Africa, South Asia, East Asia, and elsewhere might make greater contributions. The goal is to show how the international community could field up to 200,000 troops, or about twice its current capacity, for humanitarian and peace operations around the world. In addition, the study estimates what equipment, training, and rotation base would be needed to make such a force rapidly deployable, sustainable, and effective.

The implications for U.S. policy are straightforward. In terms of its own military, the United States need not make radical changes, but it should find ways to make sure that it can continue to contribute several tens of thousands of troops to humanitarian and peace operations. One approach would be to reduce the Marine Corps presence on Okinawa so that forces commonly deployed there could be deployed elsewhere if necessary. An additional approach would entail changing the Army's system for assessing the combat readiness of its forces. Specifically, forces deployed in peace operations, which have been considered unready for core national security tasks in the past, should instead be viewed as contributing to important U.S. interests. This change would encourage the Army to find better ways of making forces available for humanitarian and peace operations.

As for trying to help augment the military capabilities of other countries, Washington needs a multitiered strategy. For major U.S. allies, it primarily needs to provide political encouragement to persuade them to build smaller but more expeditionary armed forces. It also needs to recognize that its allies will expect greater influence in humanitarian and peace operations if they provide more capabilities—but that trade-off is one that the United States should be most willing to accept.

In the case of poorer countries, the United States and other western states should provide economic aid and technical assistance to help those countries improve their own national capabilities. Previous efforts along such lines, including the U.S. Africa Crisis Response Initiative, should be gradually expanded severalfold.

CHAPTER TWO

THE NEED TO DOUBLE THE GLOBAL EFFORT

How much physical military capacity does the international community need in order to mitigate the world's civil conflicts more effectively? While there is no precise answer to this question, of course, this chapter argues in broad terms that the international community should be capable of sustaining roughly twice as many forces in the field as it has tended to deploy over the past decade. Rather than effectively being limited to aggregate deployments of about 100,000 troops for humanitarian intervention and peace operations, the global community should be able to field 200,000 troops over an extended period. Allowing for the maintenance of a rotation base, that number translates into an aggregate capacity of about half a million troops capable of difficult operations abroad. Since it is unrealistic to expect the United States to provide the bulk of the necessary troops, given its other international obligations, other countries will need to develop the capacity to provide most such forces.

How can one estimate the global need for deployable, sustainable military forces? Such an estimate is inherently political and subjective, since it requires some means of assessing which conflicts the world should try to stop by force and which it should not. It is also clearly speculative, since it must make such estimates for the future, and future conflicts cannot easily be predicted.

That said, there are reasonable grounds for thinking that the world should be able to field 200,000 forces for missions of these types. One way to estimate is to examine the recent past, identifying conflicts that may have merited interventions, but for which military capacity was felt to be lacking. Another is to examine the present, making a similar assessment. Such analyses cannot possibly do justice to all the specific considerations that must factor into any actual decision to intervene or not. Instead, they are intended to be suggestive of situations where intervention should at least have been seriously considered— especially in cases where the lack of military wherewithal appears to have been a major reason why it was not.

The first step in reaching this type of estimate about desirable global intervention capacity is to recognize the obvious: it is not possible to settle every conflict in the world. Some might be exacerbated by external involvement. Some might be so intractable as not to justify the effort, money, political attention from world leaders, and blood of international soldiers that would be required to stop them. Other conflicts are not severe enough to justify forcible intervention. While they might warrant international diplomatic attention, and possibly the deployment of peacekeepers if cease-fires could be established, they do not merit deployment of many thousands of troops in a muscular mission to impose a peace or protect innocent populations. Even an ambitious proposal for stopping civil conflict must have limits, given the sheer number of conflicts—dozens by some counts—that are going on around the world today.

One attractive idea is to focus on using force to stop genocide. Speaking shortly after NATO's 1999 Kosovo war against Serbia, President Bill Clinton held out such a goal: "I think there's an important principle here that I hope will now be upheld in the future. . . . And that is that while there may well be a great deal of ethnic and religious conflict in the world— some of it might break out into wars—that whether within or beyond the borders of a country, if the world community has the power to stop it, we ought to stop genocide and ethnic cleansing."[1] Under the 1948 UN convention against genocide, moreover, the United States and other countries are obligated to take major steps—up to and including the use of force—to prevent it.

In practice, however, the convention is not such a clear guide. It defines genocide as an effort to destroy, "in whole or in part," a national, ethnic, racial, or religious group. Does that mean that a dozen ethnically motivated murders qualify? Presumably not; otherwise, there would be genocides going on all over the world all the time. Where does one draw the line?

There may also be cases in which genocide against a given people or group is not occurring, but the scale of disaster is so enormous as to make the moral case for intervention compelling nonetheless. The widespread famine and starvation that resulted from Somalia's civil war early in the 1990s is a

1. Quoted in Ivo H. Daalder and Michael E. O'Hanlon, "Unlearning the Lessons of Kosovo," *Foreign Policy*, no. 116 (Fall 1999), p. 128.

case in point. So was the famine in Sudan's civil war several years ago.

In addition, as a practical political matter, the world's major military powers will continue to have special interests in stopping conflicts that are occurring close to their own borders. Such conflicts can cause refugee flows and other spillover effects onto the territories of great powers and their neighbors, giving countries a traditional national-interest motive as well as a humanitarian rationale for intervention. For example, President Clinton's concerns about civil conflict in Haiti early in his presidency were driven in considerable part by that country's proximity to the United States and by the exodus of Haitians to the United States that resulted. Similarly, in 1989 President George Bush decided to overthrow Panamanian strongman Manuel Noriega in part because he overturned an election and presided over the murder of an American military serviceman, but also because of concerns about Panama's place in a drug trade affecting the United States. In other words, there will be times when civil conflicts have particularly compelling strategic implications for a major power willing to do something about them, in addition to humanitarian rationales for action. Mixed-motive interventions will always be a reality of international political life. That is perfectly acceptable as long as they do not lead to the neglect of terrible wars that involve no such immediate strategic interests.

There will sometimes be cases in which humanitarian intervention makes sense even when a conflict has not yet become particularly destructive. That is particularly true if a discrete and limited intervention has a reasonably good prospect of solving a problem or if a given country has a proven potential for rapidly escalating violence that makes early action advisable.[2] As with all of the above cases, however, intervention is desirable only if it has a good chance of success in the context of the specific political and military circumstances of the conflict in question.

It is important at this point to counter two objections to humanitarian interventions that are often expressed. One objection is that interventions are usually a bad idea because they stop wars before those conflicts reach their natural conclusions, when one party would be victorious and one would be the clear loser, finally compelled to accept the results of its defeat.[3] According to this line of reasoning, intervention merely postpones the resolution of conflicts, possibly reducing violence in the short term, but at the cost of equal or greater violence in the future. This argument ignores the fact that few wars naturally end in the complete extermination of one side, meaning that losers can often regroup and rekindle their armed struggle at a future date. In the course of history, most wars have not been interrupted by the acts of well-meaning outsiders, yet they have generally failed to produce lasting peace. For evidence, one need only consider most European wars before the twentieth century as well as most conflicts in the Middle East and large parts of Africa up to this day (most of which have not been directly affected by peace-keeping missions or humanitarian interventions). In fact, today's worst wars are most numerous precisely in those parts of the world, particularly Africa, where international interventions

2. Arnold Kanter, "Memorandum to the President from the 'National Security Advisor,'" in Alton Frye, ed., *Humanitarian Intervention: Crafting a Workable Doctrine* (New York: Council on Foreign Relations, 2000), pp. 5–6.

3. Edward N. Luttwak, "Give War a Chance," *Foreign Affairs*, vol. 78, no. 4 (July/August 1999), pp. 36–44.

have been the least likely and the most minimal in scope even when they have occurred.

A second objection is that parties to conflicts have become adept at appealing to international public opinion, trying to draw the outside world into their disputes as a means of advancing their own causes. According to this line of argument, such groups will sometimes seek to use violence in a calculated way for their Machiavellian political purposes, even when they know they cannot prevail on the battlefield. They will, it is alleged, deliberately provoke their enemy into committing atrocities that then spark international intervention. The minority groups might kill some of the troops or citizens of their enemies in order to cause the enemies to overreact and oppress relatively defenseless minority populations. It has been alleged, for example, that members of the Kosovo Liberation Army used precisely this tactic, with precisely the desired result, in Kosovo in 1998 and 1999. By killing Serb police, they provoked Serbs into committing ethnic cleansing operations and murder against defenseless Albanians, directly leading to NATO intervention, and in the end, victory for the Albanians.[4]

It is true that this dynamic can unfold. Indeed, such a course of events probably did occur just as the theory predicts in Kosovo.[5] But again, most of the world's worst wars of modern times have occurred in regions where outside military intervention was unlikely, and known to be unlikely by the combatants,

4. Alan J. Kuperman, "Kosovo Option: Conditional Surrender," *Washington Post*, September 25, 1998.

5. See also Timothy W. Crawford, "Pivotal Deterrence and the Kosovo War: Why the Holbrooke Agreement Failed," *Political Science Quarterly*, vol. 116, no. 4 (Winter 2001–02), pp. 497–523.

casting into doubt the notion that this effect is common. Moreover, the tactic leaves insurgent groups vulnerable to the possibility that the international community will become less sympathetic to their cause, particularly if the stronger power is reasonably restrained in its response to provocation. Had Serbia taken a more measured, counterinsurgent route to dealing with Kosovar Albanian terrorists, it might have avoided major international retribution. In individual cases, policymakers need to be sensitive to the possibility that their willingness to intervene could exacerbate a given conflict. However, that fact is hardly a strong argument against trying to reduce civil conflict—which has been prevalent in the world far longer than the modern concepts of peacekeeping and humanitarian intervention.

In summary, then, humanitarian interventions and peace operations should not be conducted for many of the world's conflicts, but they can make a major difference for the better in a number of them. Specifically, they are most likely to be advisable in the event of genocide, other mass-casualty conflicts, conflicts in the neighborhoods of great powers, or incipient conflicts that can be nipped in the bud with high confidence of success. Applying these rough guidelines to the recent past and present, how much more intervention capacity should the international community ideally possess?

How to Intervene

Figuring out how to intervene is at least as important as deciding whether to intervene. In fact, the two subjects are inherently intertwined. One cannot responsibly decide to intervene without first having a clear sense of what objectives the deployed troops would pursue and how they would pursue them.

Military forces, plans, and procedures that may be perfectly ample and capable for one type of intervention may be insufficient or inappropriate for another in that very same country. For example, a military deployment intended to ensure that relief supplies reach needy populations in Mogadishu may be ill suited to a manhunt for a given warlord; a mission to protect safe havens in Zaire may not be adequate to stop a genocide in neighboring Rwanda. To propose a candidate list of possible interventions, one must do more than identify especially serious conflicts; one must also specify, at least in broad terms, what any intervening force would do to stop or to mitigate the war in question.

Skeptics of interventions often insist on precise mission plans and exit schedules before the onset of any troop deployment. However, it is not always necessary or even practical to devise specific exit schedules before an operation begins.[6] Such schedules can be too constraining and generally wind up being overhauled even when they have been adopted. Among other shortcomings, they can give possible opponents of any peace plan an incentive to lie low for a specified period, then resume their use of violence when intervening forces have departed.

That said, countries must have a sense of what they are trying to accomplish and how they plan to do it before intervening. They do need a strategy for the overall intervention. Even if they cannot make it precise, they should have some general concept of an exit strategy—the political and military goals toward which they are working. Since the international community has no interest in maintaining permanent trusteeships around the

6. Ivo H. Daalder and Michael E. O'Hanlon, *Winning Ugly: NATO's War to Save Kosovo* (Brookings, 2000), pp. 215–16.

world, the goal must always be to end interventions, even if it may often take many years to do so. Intervening countries must also recognize the difficulty and dangers of forcible humanitarian missions, make sure they are prepared for the risks and demands, and ensure that they have adequate instruments at hand to accomplish the missions they set out for themselves.[7]

If outside countries do intervene in a civil conflict, they will generally have three kinds of options: (1) take sides, either overthrowing a regime or helping one side in a civil war defeat one or more other parties; (2) impose and then enforce a partition line between at least two main geographic zones (not simply between different militias within a given city or region); or (3) set up safe havens or humanitarian relief operations to protect a threatened population from murder and starvation.

It is important to choose wisely from this set of options and to choose clearly as well. Even if the international community chose the right time and place to intervene, it could easily go about it the wrong way, possibly taking a muddled approach that combines elements of the above three possibilities when it is usually better to select just one. For example, waffling between a limited intervention to provide food relief in Somalia and aggressively seeking to eliminate the leadership of one particular militia from the country's political scene cost eighteen American lives in October 1993. In Bosnia, declaring safe havens failed to make towns like Srebrenica anything close to safe and resulted in Serb forces taking UN peacekeepers hostage.

7. See, for example, John Hillen, *Blue Helmets: The Strategy of UN Military Operations* (London: Brassey's, 1998); see also, Colin Powell, "U.S. Forces: Challenges Ahead," *Foreign Affairs*, vol. 71, no. 5 (Winter 1992/93).

In some cases, systematic analysis of various options for intervention will point to a clear choice. In other cases, it may lead to the regrettable but inevitable conclusion that there are no promising ways to stop a severe war at acceptable risk and cost and with sufficiently good prospects for success. In still other cases, the assessment may lead to a murkier result—but it should at least sensitize the international community to the risks and the promise of various approaches to intervening in a continuing war.

How Many Forces Does the International Community Need?

Given the above guidelines and options for intervention, how often should the international community plan on using force to save lives? This question is difficult. It involves political and normative judgment about which conflicts merit forcible inter-vention. It also requires looking into the future to estimate how many wars might occur. This latter task is clearly impossible in one sense, yet essential in another.

One practical way to attempt this task is to examine recent history. The past can probably be a relatively good predictor of the future, given that the global severity of civil conflict has remained relatively constant for a number of years, in fact for several decades.[8] As a check on these findings, and as a way of focusing squarely on the present, one can also consider continu-ing civil conflicts in the world today. One can ask which of those might merit intervention if policymakers were unconstrained by

8. See Yahya Sadowski, *The Myth of Global Chaos* (Brookings, 1998), pp. 130–40; and Ted Robert Gurr, Monty G. Marshall, and Deepa Khosla, *Peace and Conflict 2001* (College Park, Md.: Center for International Development and Conflict Management, 2001), pp. 7–9.

the availability of forces and money, if they were constrained only by the difficulty of managing such missions competently and productively, in making decisions about when to use force.

The purpose of this analysis is not to draw firm conclusions about which additional interventions should have been conducted and how they should have been organized and undertaken. That exercise, inherently subjective in any case, would require far too voluminous an analysis for the purposes of this study. Rather, the following paragraphs have two purposes. First, they suggest that there may have been cases in the recent past, and in the present, where major interventions deserved serious consideration, yet apparently did not receive it, in part because of the lack of international capacity. Second, they give some rough illustration of how many international forces might have been needed to address those situations. In other words, this brief survey does not seek to resolve definitively whether specific possible interventions ought to have been undertaken, but it assumes that lack of physical military capability should not be the reason why the international community fails to seriously contemplate interventions in severe civil conflicts. It seeks to suggest a pragmatic upper bound on possible military demands for humanitarian and peace operations. That upper bound then serves as a guide in the following chapters to planning global military capabilities.

The 1990s

In the mid-1990s, there were eight extremely lethal conflicts: Sudan, Somalia, Rwanda, Burundi, Liberia, Angola, Bosnia, and Chechnya (see table 2-1). These cases accounted for more than 75 percent of all war-related deaths in the world over that time. In addition, the crisis in Haiti caused particular problems for the United States because of its location (as did the wars in the

Table 2-1. War-Related Deaths around the World: Conflicts with an Annual Death Rate of 1,000 or More as of Mid-1996

Country or region	Major cause of casualties	Total deaths to date	Annual death rate	Death rate ratio to U.S. murder rate[a]	Thousands of fighters[b]
Afghanistan 1990–	Civil war	15,000+	5,000	3:1	50
Algeria 1992–	Insurgency	40,000	5,000	2:1	150 vs. 12
Azerbaijan 1990–	War, Nagorno-Karabakh	10,000+	1,500	2:1	56 vs. 10
Burundi 1993–	Acts of genocide	150,000	50,000	80:1	15
India 1982–	Insurgency in Kashmir	10,000+	1,000	1:5 (in Kashmir)	n.a.
Liberia 1989–	Civil war	150,000	10,000	40:1	15 vs.10
Burma/Myanmar 1993–	War against two insurgencies	1,000+	1,000	1:5	286 vs. 20
Russia 1994–	War against Chechen resistance	30,000+	20,000+	150:1 (in Chechnya)	40 vs. 5
Rwanda 1994–	Genocide, war, then sporadic warfare	500,000+	1,000	1:1	40 vs. 20

Somalia 1991–	Civil war	350,000	1,000	1:1	10 vs. 10
Sri Lanka 1976–	War against Tamil insurgency	30,000+	2,000	1:1	126 vs. 8
Sudan 1955–	Civil war	1 million+	5,000	1.5:1	81 vs. 40
Tajikistan 1992–	War against Muslim insurgency	20,000	2,000	3:1	25 vs. 10
Turkey 1984–	War against Kurd insurgency	15,000+	3,000	1:2	600 vs. 10

Table is from Stephen J. Solarz and Michael E. O'Hanlon, "Humanitarian Intervention: When Is Force Justified?" *The Washington Quarterly* (Autumn 1997), p. 5.

Sources: Stockholm International Peace Research Institute, *SIPRI Yearbook 1995* (Oxford: Oxford University Press, 1995), pp. 28–35; International Institute for Strategic Studies, *The Military Balance 1995/96* (Oxford: Oxford University Press, 1995); Human Rights Watch, *Human Rights Watch World Report 1996* (New York: Human Rights Watch, 1995); United States Mission to the United Nations, "Global Humanitarian Emergencies, 1996" (New York: UN, February 1996); Amnesty International, *Amnesty International Report 1995* (New York: Amnesty International, 1995); Francis M. Deng, "Negotiating a Hidden Agenda: Sudan's Conflict of Identities," in I. William Zartman, ed., *Elusive Peace* (Washington, D.C.: Brookings Institution, 1995), p. 99; Chaim Kaufmann, "Possible and Impossible Solutions to Ethnic Civil Wars," *International Security* 20, no. 4 (Spring 1996), p. 160; Kevin O'Prey, *Keeping the Peace in the Borderlands of Russia*, Occasional Paper 24 (Washington, D.C.: Henry Stimson Center, 1995), pp. 30–41.

a. Ratio compares per capita death rate during conflict with annual U.S. murder rate (approximately 1,000 per 10 million).

b. The column for numbers of fighters shows government forces first.

Balkans for NATO countries), and the disastrous policies of the North Korean government led to a massive famine in that country. The international community did intervene substantially in Somalia, Haiti, and Bosnia. It also devoted some belated and limited effort to addressing the consequences of the 1994 war in Rwanda, helping refugees who fled to then-Zaire. What about the other cases, particularly those involving very large numbers of victims?

As a practical matter, the international community must weigh the risks of intervention against the likely future benefits. Intervening to stop Russia from killing tens of thousands of innocent Chechens, for instance, could have caused a major-power conflict between nuclear-weapons states and was not a viable option (just as intervening in Tibet or Kashmir against the wishes of China, India, or Pakistan would not have been an option). Invading North Korea to bring food to its starving people could have precipitated all-out war on the peninsula.

When the collateral risks are low and the humanitarian stakes are high, the case for intervention is much stronger. In Rwanda the sheer scale of the killing—nearly one million dead in several months' time in 1994—made the argument for intervention compelling. There is a very strong case that the international community should have quickly sent at least 10,000 and better yet 15,000 troops, the minimum prudent number given the size of the population and the size of the likely opposition, to defeat the genocidal Hutu militias that targeted Tutsis and moderate Hutus. Whether those forces then stayed on for years to help the country rebuild or took the radical step of partitioning Rwanda would in this urgent case have been a secondary concern and could have been debated over ensuing weeks and months, provided that some solution was found that would have reduced the chances of future killing.

Other humanitarian crises illustrate the potential scope for intervention. In Sudan in the early 1990s, hundreds of thousands died of a famine that was exacerbated by warfare between north and south.[9] In Liberia, the number of victims in the civil war during the first half of the 1990s was much smaller than in Rwanda or Sudan. But the violence was very severe on a per capita basis.[10]

Had the international community intervened in Rwanda, Sudan, and/or Liberia, it would have had one to three additional major interventions under way at a time. They would have taken place in relatively small countries, but each would have required substantial numbers of troops, in addition to those simultaneously deployed to missions in places such as Bosnia, Somalia, and Haiti over the time period in question.

How many military personnel would have been enough? It is difficult to say with precision, absent a detailed study of each country's geography and military balances as well as a detailed specification of the mission that would have been carried out in each situation. Nevertheless, several rules of thumb allow rough estimates. First, based on both military doctrine and political symbolism, intervening forces should generally be comparable in number to the largest likely internal foe they might face. With comparable numbers, as well as superior skills, mobility, and firepower, intervening forces would then

9. For very thoughtful commentary on Sudan, see Francis M. Deng, "Africa and the New World Dis-Order," *Brookings Review*, vol. 11, no. 2 (Spring 1993), pp. 32–35; Francis M. Deng, "The Sudan: Stop the Carnage," *Brookings Review*, vol. 12, no. 1 (Winter 1994), pp. 6–11.

10. See for example, Terrence Lyons, *Voting for Peace: Postconflict Elections in Liberia* (Brookings, 1998).

be well placed to dominate the ensuing battles.[11] Second, experiences with counterinsurgency and stability operations suggest that in difficult missions an intervening force may need at least 2 to 3 soldiers—and possibly even 10 or more—for every 1,000 members of a country's civilian population.[12] The populations of Liberia, Rwanda, and Sudan were roughly 3 million, 8 million, and 28 million during the mid-1990s. These rules of thumb would imply forces of more than 5,000, 15,000, and 50,000 troops, respectively. The latter figure might not have been needed to impose a partition in Sudan, for example, since that would not have required establishing control of the entire territory and providing local security for the entire population of the country. But given the width of Sudan, as well as the large size of its armed forces (more than 100,000 troops), 20,000 to 30,000 military personnel would have been called for. Forces of that size could have been required in each place for anywhere from two years to ten years, given the recent range of international experience with such efforts.

The international community deployed on average some 50,000 peacekeepers around the world on official UN missions in the 1990s and another 50,000 on average in the Balkans in the second half of the decade (see figure 2-1). The above illustrative cases suggest that anywhere from 5,000 to perhaps 50,000 more troops could have been needed over at least part of the same time period. In other words, the international community's typical aggregate deployment in the

11. See James J. Gallagher, *Low-Intensity Conflict: A Guide for Tactics, Techniques, and Procedures* (Harrisburg, Pa.: Stackpole Books, 1992), pp. 43–73.

12. James T. Quinlivan, "Force Requirements in Stability Operations," *Parameters*, vol. 25, no. 4 (Winter 1995–96), pp. 59–69.

Figure 2-1. UN Peacekeeping Forces in Official UN-Run Missions, 1993–2002ᵃ

Thousands

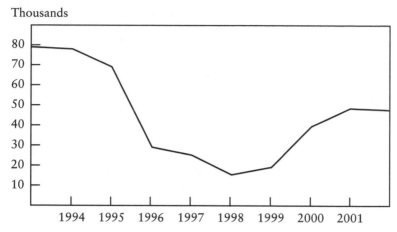

Source: Peace and Security Section of the Department of Public Information in cooperation with the Department of Peacekeeping Operations, United Nations. www.un.org/depts/dpko/dpko/contributors/30042002.pdf.

a. As of April 30, 2002.

mid-1990s—roughly 100,000 troops for peace operations and humanitarian interventions—could have been as great as 150,000 based on possible intervention in these three additional cases alone.

2002

A survey of conflicts under way in the first half of 2002, at the time of this writing, suggests the potential need for even more forces than the survey of the mid-1990s, given the situations in Congo and Afghanistan in addition to continuing NATO and UN missions (and not counting a possible postwar occupation of Iraq).

UN peacekeeping operations now involve substantially fewer troops than in the early to mid-1990s. That said, operations

Table 2-2. Current UN Peacekeeping Operations as of Mid-2002

Mission	Location	Year started	Actual troop strength[a]	Authorized troop strength	Cost (US$ millions)[b]
MONHUC	Democratic Republic of the Congo	1999	3,719	5,537	581.93
UNMEE	Eritrea and Ethiopia	2000	4,154	4,200	206.3
UNAMSIL	Sierra Leone	1999	17,275	17,500	717.6
MINURSO	Western Sahara	1991	255	n.a.	50.5
UNMISET	East Timor	May 2002	5,847	5,000	316.1
UNMOGIP	India-Pakistan border	1949	44	n.a.	6.2
UNMIBH	Bosnia and Herzegovina	1995	1,530	2,057	78.54
UNFICYP	Cyprus	1964	1,241	n.a.	42.4
UNOMIG	Georgia	1993	108	n.a.	27.9
UNMOP	Croatia and Yugoslavia	1996	27	n.a.	78.54[c]
UNDOF	Syrian Golan Heights	1974	1,030	n.a.	35.7
UNIKOM	Iraq/Kuwait	1991	1,103	n.a.	52.8
UNIFIL	Southern Lebanon	1978	3,642	n.a.	143.9
UNTSO	Middle East	1948	155	n.a.	23.2

Source: United Nations Department of Public Information as of June 2002, www.un.org/depts/dpko/dpko/cu_mission/body.htm.

n.a. Not available.

a. Troop strength includes military troops, civilian police, and military observers. It does not include local civilian staff.

b. Cost represents the amount appropriated for the current year.

c. Although an independent mission, UNMOP draws its administrative and budgetary support from UNMIBH. The General Assembly appropriated an amount of $78.54 million gross for the maintenance of UNMIBH for the period from July 1, 2002, to June 30, 2003.

Table 2-3. NATO Peacekeeping Operations in the Balkans

Mission	Troops	Participating nations
SFOR	18,000	Belgium, Canada, Czech Republic, Denmark, France, Germany, Greece, Hungary, Italy, Netherlands, Norway, Poland, Portugal, Spain, Turkey, United Kingdom, United States, Albania, Argentina, Austria, Bulgaria, Estonia, Ireland, Finland, Latvia, Lithuania, Slovakia, Morocco, Romania, Russia, Slovenia, Sweden, Australia, New Zealand
KFOR	50,000	Belgium (800), Canada (?), Czech Republic (500), Denmark (500), France (7,300), Germany (5,045), Greece (1,514), Hungary (324), Iceland (?), Italy (5,000), Luxembourg (26), The Netherlands (1,456), Norway (980), Poland (?), Portugal (295), Spain (1048), Turkey (940), United Kingdom (?), United States (5,300), Argentina (60), Austria (460), Azerbaijan (34), Bulgaria (37), Estonia (?), Finland (820), Georgia (34), Ireland (?), Lithuania (?), Morocco (500), Romania (86), Russia (?), Slovakia (40), Slovenia (6) Sweden (750), Switzerland (160), Ukraine (?), UAE (?)

Source: Stabilization Force Bosnia and Herzegovina as of March 6, 2002. www.nato.int/sfor/organisation/sfororg.htm. Kosovo Force website accessed May 30, 2002. www.nato.int/kfor/kfor/structure.htm and www.nato.int/kfor/kfor/nations/default.htm.

such as those in Sierra Leone and East Timor have kept numbers above 40,000 (see table 2-2). The international community continues to deploy almost 70,000 troops in the Balkans under NATO auspices (see table 2-3). It also now deploys about 5,000 troops in Afghanistan, specifically, in the capital city of Kabul, as part of the international security assistance force (ISAF), separate from forces still conducting Operation

THE NEED TO DOUBLE THE EFFORT

Table 2-4. Contributions to the International Security Assistance Force in Afghanistan, Early 2002

Nation	Contribution size	Mission role
Austria	60	Peacekeeping troops
Belgium	C-130 Aircraft	Transport
Britain	1,800	Peacekeeping troops, engineers, medical, logistics, policing, and air transport support
Bulgaria	20	Logistical support
Denmark	48	Peacekeeping troops, explosive ordnance disposal
Finland	50	Civil operations
France	550	Peacekeeping troops, engineers, medical personnel
Germany	800–1,000	Peacekeeping troops, infantry support
Greece	124	Peacekeeping troops, engineers, security agents
Italy	350	Peacekeeping troops, engineers, air transport
Netherlands	150	Peacekeeping troops
New Zealand	25	Supplementary peacekeeping troops
Norway	50–70	Peacekeeping troops
Portugal	25	Transport, medical, and aid workers for humanitarian mission
Romania	48	Policing and air transport support
Spain	700	Peacekeeping troops, logistics, helicopter, engineering, air transport, and explosives ordnance disposal support
Sweden	45	Information specialists
Turkey	Up to 800–1,000	Peacekeeping troops and command staff
Total	Up to 6,065	

Source: Center for Defense Information Terrorism Project, February 21, 2002. www.cdi.org/terrorism/isaf.cfm.

Enduring Freedom in that country (see tables 2-4 and 2-5). A small operation in the Sinai continues as well (see table 2-6). So the overall baseline of humanitarian and peace operations is at least as great as in the 1990s.

In Afghanistan, given the limited reach of the Karzai-led government, there is a strong case that the reach of ISAF is not nearly sufficient at present and that it should be extended to most of the rest of the country.[13] Advocates of a larger force often suggest that about 25,000 troops could do the job nationwide. In fact, such a force would be small given the size of Afghanistan. Just consider that the international community sent more than 50,000 troops to Bosnia, a small country with only one-fifth the population of Afghanistan, after the war ended in 1995; today, nearly 20,000 troops remain. To Kosovo, with less than half the area and population of Bosnia, NATO and its partners sent 50,000 troops in 1999.[14]

If 25,000 troops were deployed throughout Afghanistan, only a couple thousand could be stationed in any large city and its immediate environs. This means they would be outnumbered, since the warlords running those cities typically each control fighting forces several thousand strong. Unlike the situation of the international force in Kabul, foreign troops would not have the 10,000 combat troops (mostly at Bagram air base) at hand to help in a pinch. The force would generally need to work with the local militias. The international community would need to use the additional tools of diplomacy, suasion, and economic incentives rather than military threats in most cases to ensure their cooperation.

However, with the right mixture of military, political, and economic leverage exercised throughout Afghanistan, several thousand troops in each major province could accomplish much. Such a capability could help protect political leaders,

13. International Crisis Group, "Securing Afghanistan: The Need for More International Action," Brussels, Belgium, March 15, 2002, available at www.crisisweb.org.

14. Roberta Cohen and Michael O'Hanlon, "Send Stronger 'Stability Force' to Afghanistan," *Baltimore Sun*, June 14, 2002.

Table 2-5. Primary Contributors to Operation Enduring Freedom in Afghanistan as of early 2002

Nation	Contribution[a]
Australia	Deployed Special Operations Forces, C-130 aircraft to provide tactical lift, fighter aircraft to perform combat air patrols at the British base at Diego Garcia, and ships to support maritime operations. Australia was to deploy two KC-135 tankers to Manas, Kyrgyzstan, and the Royal Australian Air Force was slated to fill a key wing leadership position there.
Bahrain	Deployed a naval liaison officer to U.S. Naval Forces Central Command; sent a frigate to support naval missions in the region and fighter aircraft to provide combat air patrols to protect national and coalition forces in Bahrain.
Canada	Contributed 2,259 Canadian service members in CENTCOM's area of responsibility. Naval forces taking part in maritime interdiction operations, escort duties, and maritime surveillance. Canadian Air Force CC-150 Polaris and three CC-130 Hercules aircraft conducted strategic and tactical airlift.
Czech Republic	Sent three representatives to CENTCOM and about 250 personnel to Camp Doha, Kuwait, to perform local training as well consequence management support throughout the region.
France	Coalition airlift support and aerial refueling. Six Mirage 2000 fighter aircraft deployed to Manas in February. France also provided airfield security. Early in the mission a French infantry company deployed to Mazar-e-Sharif to provide area security. France provided its only carrier battle group to support combat operations in the North Arabian Sea. France has also contributed about 24 percent of its naval forces to the operation.
Germany	Deployed about 2,250 personnel to CENTCOM's area of responsibility, including special operations forces in Afghanistan. The German navy has had three frigates, a fast patrol boat group, and three supply ships operating out of Djibouti. A German air transport element has supported the task force operating out of Uzbekistan. Germany contributed 10 million euros to help train and equip the Kabul police force.

Great Britain	The British deployed their largest naval task force since the Falklands War. They provided the only coalition Tomahawk Land Attack Missile platforms to launch missiles at the start of hostilities. The Royal Air Force provided aircraft that took part in combat sorties, as well as aerial refueling, airborne early warning and intelligence, surveillance, and reconnaissance assets. British ground forces have taken part in Operation Enduring Freedom. About 40 Commandos and Royal Marines deployed to Kabul, where they have contributed to mine clearing operations.
Italy	Provided its only carrier battle group to support combat operations in the North Arabian Sea. The Italians deployed more than 13 percent of their naval forces for use in Operation Enduring Freedom. Italy is scheduled to deploy a C-130 aircraft to Manas, and has committed personnel to Operation Enduring Freedom.
Japan	Dispatched three destroyers and two supply ships with about 1,200 personnel to the Indian Ocean, where they provided at-sea refueling to U.S. and British naval vessels. About half of Japan's C-130 fleet and U-4 aircraft provided airlift support to Operation Enduring Freedom.
The Netherlands	Two Dutch naval frigates operated in CENTCOM's area of responsibility. Other naval ships, along with air force P-3s, relieved U.S. units in the Caribbean.
Romania	Approving basing and over-flight permission for U.S. and coalition partners and was planning to contribute infantry units, mine clearing equipment, and engineers to support Operation Enduring Freedom.
Spain	The Spanish were slated to deploy a P-3B to Djibouti, three C-130s to Manas, and two naval frigates to UCENTCOM.
Turkey	Provided critical KC-135 aerial refueling support for U.S. aircraft during their transit to the CENTCOM area, and basing and over-flight permission for U.S. and coalition forces.

Source: "United Against Terrorism," *The American Forces Press Service*, March 2002. www.defendamerica.mil/articles/mar2002/a030402a.html.

a. When unavoidable, figures may include contributions to the International Security Assistance Force.

Table 2-6. Sinai Multinational Force Operation[a]

Nation	Total personnel	Role
Australia	24	Provide force headquarters unit, staff appointments to force headquarters.
Canada	28	Provide air traffic control cell, staff appointments to force headquarters.
Colombia	358	Perform observation duties in central sector, North Camp security, staff appointments to force headquarters.
Fiji	339	Perform observation duties in Zone C northern sector, staff appointments to force headquarters.
France	17	Provide fixed-wing aviation unit, staff appointments to force headquarters.
Italy	83	Provide maritime support to patrol the Gulf of Aqaba and Strait of Tiran, staff appointments to force headquarters.
Hungary	39	Provide a military police unit, staff appointments to force headquarters.
New Zealand	24	Provide training and advisory team, staff appointments to force headquarters.
Norway	4	Staff appointments to force headquarters.
Uruguay	64	Provide transportation and engineering unit.
United States	985	Staff appointments to force headquarters. Provide logistic support including medical, explosive ordinance demolition, rotary wing, transportation, veterinary, sanitation, water quality, waste disposal, and incineration services throughout the force area. Perform observation duties in southern sector, including Tiran Island. USBATT is responsible for the operation of South Camp and as such performs functions that are shared by several units at North Camp.
Total[b]	1,965	

Source: The Canadian Contingent Multinational Force and Observers, http://users.actcom.co.il/~ccmfo/index.html and www. mfo.org/main.htm (modified in April 2001 and accessed in May 2002).

a. The Multinational Force and Observers is an independent peacekeeping operation begun in 1982. It is not associated with the United Nations. The MFO is funded primarily by Egypt, Israel, and the United States. The current commander is Robert Meating of Canada, who assumed command on March 1, 2001.

b. Total does not include direct-hire civilians or employees of contracted companies who serve the contingents.

especially those who might disagree with local warlords. It could deter generalized violence, banditry, and attacks on women. It could ensure fair distribution of relief supplies, even to returning refugees and internally displaced persons who do not share the ethnic identity of local authorities. It could help protect aid workers, Afghani and foreign alike, as they try to return to more of Afghanistan's remote villages. And it could be a liaison between Afghanistan's local militias, on the one hand, and its fledgling national army on the other—providing training in military tactics as well as proper human rights behavior.[15]

The conflict in Congo merits a serious debate about the pros and cons of a major peace operation. To date, the international community has chosen to hope that a minimal observer mission of about 3,000 personnel rather than a muscular peace enforcement operation will suffice there.[16] There is some chance that approach will work, given the occasionally promising sounds coming from peace negotiations sponsored by South Africa, but as of this writing it is far too soon to be confident. Meanwhile, death tolls in Congo had increased by more than half a million persons a year due to the nearly complete breakdown of the state and resulting famine and disease in the late 1990s.[17]

15. See also William J. Durch, "A Realistic Plan to Save Afghanistan," *Washington Post*, July 30, 2002, p. A17.

16. See International Crisis Group, "From Kabila to Kabila: Prospects for Peace in the Congo," ICG Africa Report no. 27, Brussels, Belgium, March 16, 2001, pp. 5–6.

17. See Les Roberts and others, "Mortality in Eastern Democratic Republic of Congo," International Rescue Committee, 2001; "Heart of Darkness: Part One—War in the Congo," *Nightline*, January 21, 2002; Marc Lacey, "Congo Tires of War, but the End Is Not in Sight," *New York Times*, July 15, 2002, p. A3; and "Africa's Great War: A Report from Congo," *The Economist*, July 6, 2002, pp. 43–45.

A mission in Congo to monitor and enforce a cease-fire line and simultaneously maintain order throughout much of the country could easily require 100,000 troops itself, using the force-sizing criteria noted above and making reference as well to the sheer magnitude and challenging topography of that country.[18] Even a mission sized by the less ambitious criteria discussed above for an expanded ISAF force in Afghanistan or focused on the eastern part of Congo where the civil conflict has been most severe (and the threat of the Rwanda Hutu *genocidaires* most enduring) could number 30,000 to 50,000 troops.

All told, therefore, the combination of continuing missions in the Balkans, Sierra Leone, and elsewhere, together with much larger stability forces in Afghanistan and Congo than are now being fielded, could push total demands for international peacekeepers to the 200,000 level. Precise figures would depend on

18. Some estimates have suggested that the total military manpower involved in Congo's recent civil war has totaled as many as 150,000 fighters. However, more recent estimates put the size of the two largest rebel groups, Rwandan Hutu (largely the *interahamwe* who led that country's 1994 genocide) and Burundian Hutu, at 15,000 and 10,000, respectively. See International Crisis Group, "Scramble for the Congo: Anatomy of an Ugly War," ICG Africa Report no. 26, Brussels, Belgium, December 20, 2000, p. 4; International Crisis Group, "Disarmament in the Congo: Investing in Conflict Prevention," Africa Briefing, Brussels, Belgium, June 12, 2001, pp. 2–3. Those latter estimates suggest that if governments agreed to a cease-fire or peace plan but rebels did not, roughly 25,000 intervening forces might suffice. However, the magnitude of Congo's territory and the size of its population—now roughly 50,000,000—point to much higher numbers, with 100,000 troops being a conservative estimate based on the rule that it is usually necessary to deploy at least 2 security personnel for every 1,000 indigenous civilians.

the specific nature of any interventions that were actually approved and undertaken, of course, but requirements would surely exceed 150,000, at a bare minimum, if those two missions were made more robust.

These figures do not include the rotational base needed to sustain a given force in the field over an extended period of time, discussed below. These estimates apply, instead, to requirements for fielded forces at a given moment.

This illustrative list, while highlighting some of the world's most vicious and lethal conflicts of recent times, does not exhaust the possible claims on intervention and peacekeeping forces. Missions might be envisioned in the future in Angola, Burundi, Sudan, Somalia, and even Indonesia—were political circumstances to change somewhat in any of these countries. The case of Burundi may be particularly plausible in the near future, given the international community's conviction that a tragedy like the 1994 Rwanda genocide must not be allowed to occur and Burundi's proven potential for interethnic violence, which might also become extremely severe under some circumstances.[19]

It is at least remotely possible that the international community could find itself in places that now seem unthinkable—such as Kashmir. This point is best proven by the case of Afghanistan, which seemed an implausible place for an intervention as recently as August 2001. If political dynamics in such places evolved to the point where local parties decided to invite international forces into their neighborhoods to help stabilize them, missions that seem entirely implausible today could become not

19. For a sobering assessment of Burundi's potential for violence, see International Crisis Group, "Burundi: Breaking the Deadlock," Africa Report No. 29, Brussels, Belgium, May 14, 2001.

only possible, but even likely. Even if operations were limited to smaller countries or localized regions of larger ones, serious efforts would generally each require at least 10,000 to 20,000 troops if outside forces were needed to forcibly impose a peace and retaliate severely against any who would challenge them.[20] Since an operation, once begun, would typically last at least two years and often longer, it is plausible that several large missions could go on at once. Indeed, the typical mission of the 1990s did last anywhere from eighteen months to several years.

Requirements for Police

How many of the total proposed pool of 200,000 security personnel should be military police, as opposed to combat troops? Although this is but one question about the detailed composition of the forces needed for the job, it is a central question, because military and police forces come from very different traditions and very different institutions. Of that total of 200,000

20. For example, the secessionist conflict in Aceh, a small and troubled province of Indonesia, involves some 3,000 guerrillas against a population base of 4.3 million. Sizing an intervention force to the guerrilla force would suggest deploying at least 3,000 troops; sizing it relative to the population base would suggest 10,000. In Burundi, similar force-sizing criteria would suggest that at least 25,000 intervening troops might be needed. See Kelly M. Greenhill, "On Intervention to Deter Deadly Conflict: A Cautionary Prospective Analysis," *Breakthroughs*, vol. 10, no. 1 (Spring 2001), pp. 36–44; Rohan Gunaratna, "The Structure and Nature of GAM," *Jane's Intelligence Review* (April 2001), pp. 33–35; Quinlivan, "Force Requirements in Stability Operations"; O'Hanlon, *Saving Lives with Force*, pp. 38–42.

personnel who might be needed around the world at any given time, some fraction would focus on logistics, some on command, control, and communications, and many on general-purpose infantry soldiering. Most of these latter specialists would still be soldiers; by contrast, police generally come from different types of organizations, whose sources of funding are different. Thus it is useful to try to get a rough sense of how many police officers might be needed.

Clearly, most of the total of 200,000 personnel should be soldiers, since establishing basic control and order is the first priority in countries wracked by extreme conflict. However, efforts to arrest war criminals, to restore criminal justice systems, and generally to institute a rule of law that would make possible the safe departure of intervening forces ultimately require some type of policing. Such policing is difficult, particularly for a multinational force drawn from various policing and legal traditions. Preparations are therefore desirable to develop a pool of well-trained police officers large enough to provide sufficient personnel when needed.[21] Although infantry soldiers can sometimes substitute for police in a pinch, that is generally not the preferred approach, because their skills are different. Soldiers are trained to deal with larger outbreaks of violence rather than to maintain order through a system of law.[22]

How many police are enough? One example is that, at present, police make up some 10 percent of the international

21. United States Institute of Peace, "American Civilian Police in UN Peace Operations," special report, Washington, D.C., July 6, 2001.

22. Annika S. Hansen, *From Congo to Kosovo: Civilian Police in Peace Operations*, International Institute for Strategic Studies, Adelphi Paper 343 (Oxford, England: Oxford University Press, 2002), p. 53.

community's security presence in Bosnia, or about 2,000 offi-cers.[23] Taking that approach, one might estimate that 20,000 police officers would be needed in a total pool of 200,000 deployed forces.

Is Bosnia a good example of likely needs in other missions? Perhaps not. International personnel for other missions in the mid-1990s typically comprised no more than 5 percent police.[24] However, UN-run missions around the world in mid-2001 included some 8,000 police—about 20 percent of all deployed forces.[25] In fact, were it not for a shortage of available police, numbers might have been even higher; in August 2000, for example, 25 percent of all authorized police positions were vacant.[26] Similarly, police composed about 15 percent of total international personnel for the Cambodia mission of the early 1990s. These latter figures suggest that a total pool of 200,000 security personnel might include as many as 30,000 to 40,000 police officers (see figure 2-2).[27]

23. Colum Lynch, "Misconduct, Corruption by U.S. Police Mar Bosnia Mission," *Washington Post*, May 29, 2001, p. A1; and United Nations, "Monthly Summary of Contributors," April 30, 2001, avail-able at www.un.org/depts/dpko/contributors/apr.htm.

24. See Harry Broer and Michael Emery, "Civilian Police in U.N. Peacekeeping Operations," in Robert B. Oakley, Michael J. Dziedzic, and Eliot M. Goldberg, *Policing the New World Disorder: Peace Operations and Public Security* (Washington, D.C.: National Defense University Press, 1998), p. 372; and United Nations, *United Nations Peacekeeping Information Notes* (December 1994), p. 242.

25. Lakhdar Brahimi and others, *Report of the Panel on United Nations Peace Operations* (New York: United Nations, 2000), p. 20.

26. Hansen, *From Congo to Kosovo*, p. 48.

27. James A. Schear and Karl Farris, "Policing Cambodia: The Public Security Dimensions of U.N. Peace Operations," in Oakley,

Figure 2-2. Civilian Police in UN Peacekeeping Operations, 1991–2002ª

Number of civilian police

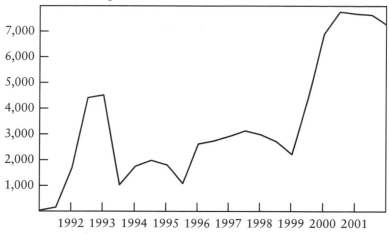

Source: Peace and Security Section of the Department of Public Information in cooperation with the Department of Peacekeeping Operations, United Nations. www.un.org/depts/dpko/dpko/contributors/30042002.pdf.
  a. As of April 30, 2002.

All things considered, increasing available police capacity by at least 10,000 police officers, above and beyond existing numbers, should be seen as a minimum objective. An ideal target might be to earmark and train 20,000 additional officers, or nearly 15,000 more than are presently being organized under the European Union initiative to create an available pool of 6,000 police personnel.

Dziedzic, and Goldberg, *Policing the New World Disorder*, p. 82; United Nations, *United Nations Peacekeeping Information Notes* (New York: United Nations, 1993), p. 52.

As for the question of who should "own" these assets and what the additional officers should do when not deployed, several approaches might be taken. Expanding that pool of EU police might be part of the answer. Asking individual countries to add modest numbers of military police to their military force structures (in lieu of some existing infantry troops) might be another part. Creating "police reserves" made up of retired officers or individuals with other peacetime jobs might be a third mechanism.

Summary

In conclusion, UN and NATO missions combined have typically involved about 100,000 troops over the past decade. They have done good work in certain places but little in others, partly because deploying 100,000 troops so taxed the international community's military capacities that additional missions were difficult to contemplate even when potentially quite necessary.

Were military capacity not such a severe constraint, the international community might well have been willing to intervene in a number of additional conflicts, including Rwanda, Sudan, and Liberia in the mid-1990s, as well as the Congolese conflict more recently. Based just on cases considered here, total force requirements could quite easily have reached 150,000 individuals at a time, and perhaps 200,000, of which some 30,000 to 40,000 individuals would ideally have been police personnel and the rest military troops.

The above figures do not include the need for a larger rotational base of personnel. In sustained operations, a soldier cannot be expected to spend more than one year out of every three or so on deployment, given the need for time at home, for training, and for service to his or her own national armed forces. As discussed below, that means the world community should ideally possess more than half a million deployable military and police personnel for addressing conflicts around the world.

CHAPTER THREE

PROJECTABLE MILITARY FORCES IN THE WORLD TODAY

Taken together, the world's nations spend the equivalent of $800 billion a year on military forces and keep twenty-two million men and women under arms in their armed forces. However, only a modest percent of those financial resources, and only a very small fraction of those troops, translate into military force that can be deployed over substantial distances. Leaving aside the United States, which has a nearly $400 billion defense budget as well as hundreds of thousands of troops that can be deployed overseas within months and sustained abroad indefinitely, the rest of the world combined cannot muster more than about two hundred thousand military personnel for such purposes. The United Kingdom has considerable force-projection capabilities relative to its force structure and national means. But most countries, even those with strong militaries, are unable to deploy and sustain even modest fractions of their total armed forces abroad.

This situation is far from ideal. The United States has a relatively limited willingness to engage in humanitarian military interventions and peace operations. Its military, shrunk by a third since the cold war ended, is already burdened by numerous missions abroad, missions that provide benefits not just to the United States, but also to its allies and the international community more generally.[1] Its public and even more so its Congress are unwilling to stomach large numbers of casualties suffered in distant lands for missions that seem indirectly related to core national security interests and often seem less than completely successful. Moreover, despite much commentary to the contrary, the United States already contributes roughly its fair share to global humanitarian missions. The numbers of U.S. troops formally under UN command are quite small, but the United States contributes substantial numbers to the UN-approved and NATO-led operations in the Balkans. It is the lead actor in Operations Northern Watch and Southern Watch in Iraq, missions that at least initially were designed largely for humanitarian purposes, though their purposes are admittedly more strategic today. It leads Operation Enduring Freedom in Afghanistan, another mission motivated by strategic concerns that also serves humanitarian purposes. The broad point is not that the United States does enough, but that its share is already substantial and also that its share is unlikely to increase.

Indeed, military missions motivated principally by humanitarian, as opposed to traditional strategic, interests should be

1. Problems with U.S. military readiness are sometimes exaggerated, but they are real: see, for example, Jason Forrester, Michael O'Hanlon, and Micah Zenko, "Measuring U.S. Military Readiness," *National Security Studies Quarterly*, vol. 7, no. 2 (Spring 2001), pp. 99–120.

borne equitably by the international community. The United States should do its fair share, but there is no reason to assign it a special burden. Other countries can and should do more than they are doing at present. There is little reason to think that most countries would object to this argument as a matter of principle. But other countries do not generally have enough capacity for rapid, forceful intervention. Whatever their words may be, their actions to date are generally inadequate to the challenges at hand.

Before developing an agenda for action, it is necessary to document more carefully the present international state of deployable military power. This chapter does so by examining the capabilities of European countries, Japan, China, Russia, and several key regions, including Africa and South Asia.

Most countries do not present data on the sizes of their deployable military capabilities, even in their official defense posture statements or white papers. The United States provides a large amount of data on relevant capabilities; some European and western Pacific democracies provide modest amounts of information as well. Nevertheless, even for these countries, some work is needed to estimate actual military capabilities.

The methodology for estimating countries' projectable military capabilities focuses on three elements: strategic lift, logistics assets that allow units to operate in foreign regions, and properly trained and equipped combat troops. Focusing on these three issues reveals many constraints on most countries' capabilities. Many do not have long-range airlift and sealift, even if they may have some limited tactical transport capabilities for moving over short distances. Most depend on their national economies and civilian infrastructures to provide logistics support—including equipment repair, provisioning of fuel and ammunition, medical care, and food and water for troops.

As a result they are often unable to support troops that have been taken away from their home territories. Finally, many countries still depend on conscripts to fill out their force structures. Such conscripts are often poorly trained or poorly equipped. Many countries face legal or political restrictions on deploying troops, and especially conscripts, abroad as well. Whichever is the weakest of these three requirements—strategic lift, deployable logistics, and deployable, well-prepared troops—determines a country's capacity.

The estimates below focus on forces available for rapid deployment and for sustained operations abroad (see table 3-1). What are the criteria for assessing the capacity of a given military for such power projection? As a rough rule of thumb, a reasonable standard is that forces should be deployable within two to three months and then supportable in a foreign theater for an indefinite period—at least a year—thereafter. These criteria are similar to those of the European Union's "Headline Goals" initiative of 1999, which calls for the EU to be able to deploy and sustain 60,000 troops abroad. Many countries could rent sealift, call up reserves, obtain special legal authority to deploy conscripts, and take other such measures if time were not a constraint. Given the nature of most humanitarian missions, however, delays of many months are generally unacceptable. Countries are also usually reluctant to take the extreme steps mentioned above for peace and humanitarian operations in any event. For these reasons, this chapter focuses on promptly deployable and sustainable forces.

The Major Industrialized Democracies

The major western democracies collectively spend a good deal of money on defense and field quite large forces. Yet on the whole, their military capabilities for power projection are modest.

Europe

The aggregate defense budgets of NATO Europe totaled about $150 billion in 2001. That figure was down about $25 billion from 1999, a period during which the American defense budget began to grow again. Despite that decline, however, NATO Europe's military budgets still totaled almost half that of the United States in 2001. Their military manpower of roughly 2.4 million active-duty troops exceeds that of the United States by a million people.[2]

Most of Europe's potential expeditionary capability resides in eight countries, mostly in northern or western Europe, that enjoy per capita wealth comparable to that of the United States and do not face significant security problems near to home. France, Germany, and Britain have an aggregate 2001 defense budget totaling $90 billion and aggregate active-duty military manpower of about 730,000. Germany is, however, at risk of dropping out of this "big three" status; despite having the continent's largest economy, Germany has cut its defense budget by almost $10 billion in the past three years to just over $25 billion now. Italy has a $20 billion defense budget and a troop total of 250,000, similar to France, Britain, and Germany. Four smaller powers, led by the Netherlands and also including Belgium, Denmark, and Norway, have a combined 2001 defense budget of $14 billion and aggregate troop strength of 135,000.

Together these eight countries spend the equivalent of $125 billion a year on defense—more than 80 percent of the

2. International Institute for Strategic Studies, *The Military Balance 2001/2002* (Oxford, England: Oxford University Press, 2001), p. 297.

Table 3-1. The Global Supply of Projectable Military Force, 2001[a]

Country	Defense resources (US$ billions)	Ground forces (thousands)		
		Total active strength	Deployable in 1–3 months, sustainable 1 year	Percent of total quickly deployable
United States	310.5	649	400	62
United Kingdom	34	121	25	21
France	33.3	152	15	10
Germany	26.5	212	10	5
Italy	20.5	138	5	4
Canada	7.3	19	4	21
Netherlands	6.0	15	4	27
Denmark	2.4	13	1	8
Other NATO	27.3	829	20	2
Subtotal, non-U.S. NATO	157.3	1,499	84	6
NATO aspirants	1.7	120.2	...	...
European neutrals	10.5	95.4	5	1
Australia	7	24	5	21
New Zealand	1	4	0.75	19
Japan	40	149	5	3
South Korea	12	560	5	1
India	16	1,100	10	1
Pakistan	3	550	2	0.3
Bangladesh	1	120	0.3	0.3
Sri Lanka	1	95	1	1
Malaysia	2	80	2	3
Singapore	4	50	2	4

Russia	60	329	35	11
China	50	1,610	20	1
African "neutrals"	4.5	398.6	10	3
Argentina, Brazil, Chile	14	300	12	4
Non-U.S. total	385.0	about 200	about 3	1.5

Sources: International Institute for Strategic Studies, *The Military Balance* (London: Oxford University Press, 2001); and in addition:

U.K.: Ministry of Defence, *The Future Strategic Context for Defence* (London, 2001), p. 21; Ministry of Defence, *Strategic Defence Review White Paper* (London, 1998), chapter 5 and supporting essay 6, annex B, available at www.mod.uk/index. php3?page=252.

France: Ministry of Defense, *Report of Activities in 2000* (Paris, 2000), chapter on Armee de Terre, available at www.defense. gouv.fr/terre/orga/dispos/org_2002/ index.html.

Germany: Report of the Commission to the Federal Government, "Common Security and the Future of the Bundeswehr," Federal Republic of Germany, May 2000, available at www.bundeswehr.de/ministerium/politik_aktuell/zk-e1.html.

Canada: Ministry of Defense, *Defence Planning Guidance 2001* (Ottawa, 2000), pp. 3–6.

Netherlands: Ministry of Defense, *Summary of the Defense White Paper 2000* (Amsterdam, 1999).

Denmark: Danish Defence Commission, *Defence for the Future* (1997), p. 24.

Other NATO: See, for example, Ministry of National Defence, *White Paper of the Hellenic Armed Forces, 1998–1999* (Athens, Greece, 2000), section 4.1.2.8a, available at www.mod.gr/english/index.htm; Ministry of Defence, "The Long Term Defence Plan for 2002–2005: Short Version," Oslo, Norway, December 2000, pp. 4–5, available at odin.dep.no/fd/engelsk/publ/veiledninger/010011-120018/ index-dok000-b-n-a.html.

European neutrals: Council of State, *Report to Parliament* (Helsinki, 1997), pp. 78–79, available at www.vn.fi/vn/english/publicat/ 970317se.htm.

Australia: Ministry of Defence, *Defence 2000: Our Future Defence Force* (Commonwealth of Australia, 2000), pp. 80–84.

New Zealand: Ministry of Defence, *New Zealand Defence Force Capability Reviews* (Wellington, 2000), pp. 52–76; Phillip Mckinnon, "New Zealand: A Spent Force?" *Jane's Defence Weekly*, June 20, 2001, p. 48.

Japan: Japanese Defense Agency, *Defense of Japan 2000* (Tokyo, 2000), pp. 86–89.

South Korea: Ministry of National Defense, *Defense White Paper 2000* (Seoul, 2000), pp. 74–76.

a. This table essentially estimates what countries could themselves deploy and support abroad with their own immediately available strategic lift assets—primarily dedicated military airlift and sealift, as well as amphibious vessels. The estimates also include consideration of whether combat units can be supported in the field in undeveloped regions by their own organic logistics assets.

NATO Europe total. They field slightly less than half of NATO Europe's total troop strength, or 1.1 million active-duty personnel. In other words, their spending per person is relatively high by comparison with other European countries. Those broad metrics suggest that these eight countries could possess at least one-third the usable military capabilities of the United States, since their combined spending levels are about one-third of the Pentagon's and their troop strength is roughly comparable to that of the U.S. military. Yet, as shown in table 3-1, they collectively have the ability to deploy and sustain less than one-sixth of what American forces could muster. Counting the rest of Europe as well, total capacities are less than one-fourth those of the U.S. armed forces. Most other NATO countries do not have substantial power projection capabilities, though Turkey, considered in a general category below, does have some capacity.

There are various explanations of why most major western countries do not have significant capabilities for conducting military operations abroad. To begin, Germany and Italy still rely heavily on the draft to supply their forces. At first blush, this may seem a good economy. However, countries relying on conscription generally get what they pay for. The draft generally produces young conscripts who need most of their very short terms of service (typically ten to twelve months) just to learn basic skills before being discharged. They are also not legally or practically deployable overseas in many cases.[3]

3. Institute for National Strategic Studies, *1997 Strategic Assessment* (Washington, D.C.: National Defense University, 1996), p. 35; Interview with French Armed Forces Chief of Staff, General Jean-Philippe Douin, *Jane's Defence Weekly*, June 19, 1996, p. 112; John E. Peters and Howard Deshong, *Out of Area or Out of Reach? European Military Support for Operations in Southwest Asia* (Santa Monica, Calif.: RAND Corporation, 1995), p. 70; and Hans Ruhle, "The

During the cold war, many European countries did not view power projection as an important mission. The legacy of that philosophy endures today. Apart from Britain, and to a certain extent France, many European countries retain cold war–like armed forces—downsized to be sure, but still focused primarily on territorial defense rather than out-of-area operations. They also tend to remain shackled logistically to their national infra- structures and economies. The situation is changing, but the political impetus to change is limited in strength, and as a con- sequence the results are also limited.

What power can Europe project today? Over a period of days or weeks it can move several thousand troops, principally British and French, and dozens of fighter aircraft. Its real weakness would manifest itself in the period two weeks to three months after a crisis began outside the continent. During that time, the United States could deploy large amounts of equipment by using prepositioning ships, large transport aircraft, fast sealift, and then dedicated cargo and tanker ships. Europeans could deploy only some light infantry forces in that time, unless aided by U.S. strate- gic transport, and would probably get armored forces to a distant theater like the Persian Gulf only after several months. Even then, beyond a couple of divisions, they would be largely reliant on the United States for in-theater logistics support.[4]

German Bundeswehr: No Muscle for 'Out-of-Area,'" *Global Affairs*, vol. 8, no. 3 (Summer 1993), pp. 158–60.

4. For concurring European views, see Colin McInnes, "The Future of NATO," in Christoph Bluth, Emil Kirchner, and James Sperling, *The Future of European Security* (Hampshire, England: Dartmouth Publishing Company, 1995), pp. 102–03; and Commission de defense, Assemblée de l'Union de l'Europe occidentale, "Les force armées européennes," Document Numero 1468, Paris, France, 12 juin 1995, p. 7.

A good benchmark for understanding European power projection capabilities is the 1990–91 Persian Gulf War. In that conflict, the Netherlands, Norway, Belgium, Denmark, Italy, Germany, and Canada each generally provided one or two small ships, a squadron or so of aircraft, and perhaps a specialized capability like Patriot missile defense batteries. As a group, they provided essentially no ground forces, only about one wing of combat aircraft (much of it in backup mode in Turkey), and a total of around 15,000 troops. France provided somewhat more than 10,000 troops. Britain provided more forces than all the above countries combined, or about 35,000 troops. That included 28,000 soldiers in the 1st Armored Division. All told, the non-U.S. NATO contribution represented about 65,000 individuals, or just over 10 percent of total NATO forces in the Gulf.[5] The British contribution was quite respectable, adjusted for the size of that country and its military, but most other countries' efforts were not impressive.

European capabilities have not improved markedly since the Gulf War. As one indication of how things stood in the late 1990s, it was estimated that NATO countries besides the United States and United Kingdom would have been able to contribute only some 20,000 to 30,000 troops to a possible invasion of nearby Kosovo in 1999.[6] New initiatives and organizations such as the Eurocorps, Ace Rapid Reaction Corps, the Combined Joint Task Force (CJTF) concept, the Helsinki Head-

5. See Steven R. Bowman, "Persian Gulf War: Summary of U.S. and Non-U.S. Forces," Report 91-167 F, Congressional Research Service, February 11, 1991, pp. 1–20.

6. See Ivo H. Daalder and Michael E. O'Hanlon, *Winning Ugly: NATO's War to Save Kosovo* (Brookings, 2000), pp. 157–58.

line Goal for deployable military forces (see table 3-2), and the 2002 Prague initiative have pointed things in a positive direction. Moreover, France has nearly eliminated the draft, and other countries have restructured their armed forces in various ways as well.[7]

Nevertheless, transport assets are still scarce. Amphibious assault ships have the capacity to transport only about 2,600 British troops, 2,300 French troops, 2,000 Spaniards, 1,000 Italian forces, and 600 troops from the Netherlands. Additional sealift capabilities across the continent total enough capacity for perhaps a brigade-sized force. Most airlift is tactical in range and incapable of carrying large heavy equipment.[8] Despite the advent of the corps-level organizations and the CJTF concept, logistics support often remains tied to the civilian economies in home territory.[9]

The European democracies do have numerous strengths that should not be forgotten. In addition to having large numbers of proficient troops and considerable defense resources, most are willing to risk greater casualties in humanitarian and peace operations than is the United States. Britain and France lost dozens of soldiers in the UNPROFOR mission in Bosnia in the early 1990s, yet they continued the mission despite those costs and the operation's own obvious shortcomings. More recently, Britain has contributed combat troops to dangerous operations in Sierra Leone. Certain smaller powers,

7. Peters and Deshong, *Out of Area or Out of Reach?* pp. 94, 120.

8. International Institute for Strategic Studies, *The Military Balance 2001/2002*, pp. 295–98.

9. Peters and Deshong, *Out of Area or Out of Reach?* pp. 77–87, 92, 107, 120.

Table 3-2. Initial European Force Commitments[a]

Country	Ground forces	Combat aircraft[b]	Ships
Austria	2 battalions[c]	n.a.	n.a.
Belgium	1,000	n.a.	n.a.
Finland	1,430[c]	n.a.	1 mine-sweeper[c]
France	12,000	75	15
Germany	13,500	93	20
Great Britain	12,500[c]	72[c]	18[c]
Greece	4,000	n.a.	n.a.
Ireland	850[c]	n.a.	n.a.
Italy	12,000	47	19
Luxembourg	100	n.a.	n.a.
Netherlands	2 battalions	1–2 squadrons	1 frigate
	1 brigade	1 battery Patriot missiles	1 taskforce
Portugal	1,000	n.a.	n.a.
Spain	6,000	n.a.	n.a.
Sweden	1 battalion		
	1 MP company	n.a.	n.a.

Source: Thomas Skold, "States Pledge Resources for Crisis Management," *European Security Review* (December 2000); Joseph Fitchett, "EU Force Takes Shape with Pledge of Troops," *International Herald Tribune,* November 20, 2000; and John D. Morrocco, "European Union Forges Rapid Reaction Force," *Aviation Week and Space Technology,* November 27, 2000, p. 28.

a. Initial commitments made at the November 20, 2000, EU Defense Ministerial Meeting. The EU has pledged 60,000 troops for one year for a rapid reaction force by 2003. Denmark is not participating, and Austria has sought more time to consider its role. Although Turkey is not a member of the EU, it has pledged a mechanized infantry brigade, two F-16 squadrons, and two C-130s.

b. The European Union goal for combat aircraft is 350.

c. Confirmed.

such as the Scandinavian nations, take pride in their commitment to peace operations. Certain countries, such as Poland within NATO and Ukraine outside it, seem eager to contribute more as well, perhaps partly to strengthen their ties to the West. Britain, Germany, France, and Turkey have contributed large numbers of forces to the International Security Assistance Force (ISAF) operation in Afghanistan; several of those countries as well as Canada and Australia have also participated in combat operations under U.S. command there. Were some European countries to acquire greater capabilities for operating beyond their borders, they would probably use them for quite worthwhile purposes.

Canada, Australia, and New Zealand

Canada and Australia each spends about $7 billion annually on its military and each fields about 50,000 active-duty forces. New Zealand has a proud history in peacekeeping, but its capabilities are beneath those of the four small European countries mentioned above and seem to be slipping further. At this point it has become a minor actor, even by the standards of small countries.

In humanitarian interventions and peace operations, Australia in particular has an impressive recent track record. It provided most of the forces for the mission to restore stability to East Timor when the United States, Japan, and other countries proved unwilling to help much. Both Canada and Australia have, as noted above, been of considerable help to the United States in Afghanistan. They have the capacity to deploy and sustain a few thousand troops each.

Turkey and South Korea

Turkey and South Korea have somewhat similar military attributes. Both countries are close U.S. allies with relatively large and rather good militaries. Their defense budgets are each in the range of $10 billion to $13 billion, and their active-duty armed forces of more than 600,000 troops each are the largest among major U.S. allies. Turkey is a member of NATO and a European country, of course—but it is not part of the European Union or party to the Helsinki Headline Goals, so it is best considered separately from the rest of NATO in any event.

Neither Turkey nor South Korea has major ideological reservations about intervention. In fact, both have contributed in the past to multilateral missions abroad—the Turks in Korea and now Afghanistan, the Koreans in Vietnam—though these were wars in defense of core western security interests rather than purely humanitarian operations. They might be willing to participate in missions abroad again, perhaps even for strictly humanitarian purposes, though Ankara is sensitive to missions that could condone ethnic separatism, given its worries about separatism among the Kurdish population in eastern Turkey. In particular, Turkey's interest in retaining an important role in NATO will likely mean that it will continue to participate in alliance missions like those in the Balkans and Afghanistan.

However, both countries remain in particularly dangerous neighborhoods. As such, for the foreseeable future they will have limited freedom to participate in peace or humanitarian missions in distant lands.[10] They will thus tend not to invest large sums in the types of logistics and transport capabilities needed for distant operations. Modest investments may be feasible, however.

10. On South Korea's security outlook, see, for example, Sung-Han Kim, "Korea-U.S. Relations," in Institute of Foreign Affairs and National Security, *The Korean Peninsula and Korean-U.S. Relations* (Seoul: Institute of Foreign Affairs and National Security, 1997), pp. 93–106; Heinz Kramer, *A Changing Turkey: The Challenge to Europe and the United States* (Brookings, 2000), pp. 202–19.

Japan

Japan presently spends the equivalent of $40 billion to $45 billion annually on its military—more than any European country and comparable to the military expenditures of China and Russia. Despite that budget, Japan's armed forces contribute little to regional or global security.

Japan's armed forces today comprise 240,000 active-duty uniformed personnel. About 150,000 are in the army, 45,000 in the navy, and 45,000 in the air force. Another 50,000 individuals are in the reserves, almost all in the army (that is, the ground self-defense forces). Japan's military missions revolve primarily around providing defense for the nation's territory and helping to defend sea lanes and airspace extending as far as roughly 1,000 miles from Tokyo.

Leaving aside statistics, Japan's armed forces have changed little during the post–cold war era. While the United States has reduced its military strength by one-third since 1990 and European NATO countries have on average cut by one-quarter, Japan's military remains only a few percent smaller than a decade ago, and its missions and structure are quite similar. Tokyo has generally failed to follow up on its limited support for mine clearing after the Persian Gulf War or its modest role in peacekeeping in Cambodia in the early 1990s with further significant steps toward enhanced participation in multilateral overseas military operations (see table 3-3). It did send naval support ships into the Indian Ocean to support Operation Enduring Freedom. But Japan's unwillingness to put forces anywhere near harm's way in Afghanistan, the Balkans, or East Timor was nonetheless in striking contrast to the efforts of European countries.

Table 3-3. Japanese Participation in UN Peacekeeping and Humanitarian Assistance Activities, 1992–2000

Period of operation	Name of operation	Number of Japanese personnel
9/1992–10/1992	United Nations Angola Verification Mission II (UNAVEM)	3 observers
9/1992–9/1993	United Nations Transitional Authority in Cambodia (UNTAC)	49 observers; 600 military engineering personnel; 75 police
5/1993–1/1995	United Nations Operation in Mozambique (ONUMOZ)	15 observers; 53 military personnel
3/1994–4/1994	United Nations Observers Mission in El Salvador (ONUSAL)	15 observers
9/1994–12/1994	Humanitarian assistance activities in Rwanda	401 military personnel
2/1996–present	United Nations Disengagement Observer Force (INDOF)	45 military personnel
8/1998–9/1998	OSCE Mission to Bosnia and Herzegovina (monitoring of general election/municipal election)	30 observers/administrators
7/1999–9/1999	United Nations Transitional Administration in East Timor (UNTAET)	3 police
11/1999–3/2000	Evacuation operation in East Timor	113 military personnel
3/2000–4/2000	Monitoring of municipal election, OSCE Mission to Bosnia and Herzegovina	11 observers

Source: National Institute for Research Advancement, *Japan's Proactive Peace and Security Strategies,* Report No. 20000005 (Tokyo, 2001), p. 39.

Developing Countries

Developing countries are important contributors to global peace and humanitarian operations. Countries such as Jordan, Kenya, Nigeria, Ghana, Guinea, Zambia, India, Pakistan, Bangladesh, Nepal, Thailand, and the Philippines particularly have historically played key roles in peacekeeping missions.

They often stand to gain certain benefits, in the realms of financial compensation and military training, by contributing to such efforts. Some are also willing to participate in more difficult and dangerous security tasks because they generally bear the brunt of civil wars that frequently occur in their neighborhoods. Most are less casualty averse than the United States and other western countries. For all these reasons developing countries should be an important part of any blueprint for a more robust and comprehensive global approach to stopping civil conflict and its deadly consequences.

Africa

African militaries have been involved in peacekeeping missions in the past and remain involved today. However, their potential to do more to address conflicts on their own continent and in other parts of the conflict-ridden developing world will be realized only if they make significant improvements to existing capacity.

In current peacekeeping missions, African nations supply some 10,000 troops. The majority are from Nigeria, Kenya, and Ghana. Significant numbers of troops—several hundred or more per country—have also been contributed to peacekeeping missions at various times by Ethiopia, Egypt, Senegal, Guinea, Morocco, Tunisia, and Botswana. The largest mission in Africa to which these forces have deployed of late has been in Sierra Leone, though missions also exist along the Ethiopia/Eritrea border, in the western Sahara, and in Congo (see table 3-4).

On the whole, however, African militaries are not well suited to difficult operations abroad. Although sub-Saharan African countries collectively field about 1.5 million soldiers, or 7 percent of the world's total military manpower, they are supported by defense budgets that amount to just over 1 percent of total

Table 3-4. Peacekeeping Contributions as of June 30, 2002[a]

Country	Observers	Police	Troops	Total
Albania	1	. . .	. . .	1
Algeria	19	. . .	1	20
Argentina	12	176	461	649
Australia	26	94	1,150	1,270
Austria	13	54	348	415
Bangladesh	65	131	5,254	5,450
Belgium	11	2	5	18
Benin	24	1	4	29
Bolivia	10	. . .	204	214
Bosnia and Herzegovina	9	16	. . .	25
Brazil	15	12	75	102
Bulgaria	6	134	2	142
Burkina Faso	12	. . .	. . .	12
Cameroon		20	1	21
Canada	18	47	202	267
Chile	11	6	27	44
China	52	84	1	137
Croatia	15	. . .	. . .	15
Czech Republic	18	29	1	48
Denmark	38	53	4	95
Ecuador	. . .	1	. . .	1
Egypt	57	127	5	189
El Salvador	4	1	. . .	5
Estonia	1	. . .	. . .	1
Fiji	7	49	774	830
Finland	37	37	5	79
France	46	207	243	496
Gambia	19	39	2	60
Germany	11	535	14	560
Ghana	47	301	2,141	2,489
Greece	9	30	. . .	39
Guinea	14	. . .	780	794

(continued)

Table 3-4. Peacekeeping Contributions as of June 30, 2002ᵃ *(Continued)*

Country	Observers	Police	Troops	Total
Honduras	12	. . .	. . .	12
Hungary	18	18	119	155
Iceland	. . .	6	. . .	6
India	37	606	2,379	3,022
Indonesia	29	21	3	53
Ireland	30	55	267	352
Italy	30	93	206	329
Japan	. . .	. . .	679	679
Jordan	44	638	1,091	1,773
Kenya	55	57	1,747	1,859
Kyrgyzstan	2	. . .	. . .	2
Lithuania	. . .	9	. . .	9
Malawi	18	21	. . .	39
Malaysia	61	121	43	225
Mali	29	2	3	34
Morocco	. . .	. . .	657	657
Mozambique	4	6	. . .	10
Namibia	3	. . .	3	6
Nepal	36	53	966	1,055
Netherlands	12	55	3	70
New Zealand	15	. . .	723	738
Niger	11	12	1	24
Nigeria	56	75	3,320	3,451
Norway	22	49	7	78
Pakistan	76	343	4,398	4,817
Paraguay	19	. . .	1	20
Peru	5	. . .	. . .	5
Philippines	8	151	56	215
Poland	22	176	822	1,020
Portugal	. . .	90	678	768
Republic of Korea	14	. . .	456	470
Romania	39	203	1	243
Russian Federation	91	164	112	367

(continued)

Table 3-4. Peacekeeping Contributions as of June 30, 2002ᵃ *(Continued)*

Country	Observers	Police	Troops	Total
Samoa	. . .	33	. . .	33
Senegal	16	59	479	554
Singapore	4	25	65	94
Slovak Republic	4	. . .	596	600
Slovenia	2	17	. . .	19
South Africa	7	. . .	147	154
Spain	5	158	3	166
Sri Lanka	. . .	73	. . .	73
Sweden	33	87	1	121
Switzerland	20	17	1	38
Tanzania	20	2	3	25
Thailand	18	36	364	418
Tunisia	22	. . .	263	285
Turkey	13	168	. . .	181
Ukraine	27	230	1,273	1,530
United Kingdom	34	246	427	707
United States	33	646	1	680
Uruguay	71	. . .	1,494	1,565
Vanuatu	. . .	6	. . .	6
Venezuela	3	. . .	. . .	3
Zambia	30	53	840	923
Zimbabwe	. . .	87	. . .	87
Total	1,787	7,153	36,402	45,342

Source: Peace and Security Section of the Department of Public Information in cooperation with the Department of Peacekeeping Operations, United Nations. www.un.org/depts/dpko/dpko/contributors/jun02.htm.

a. The figures do not include UN-authorized missions that are run by non-UN entities, such as NATO in the Balkans. Current UN missions include missions in Democratic Republic of the Congo, Eritrea and Ethiopia, Sierra Leone, Western Sahara, East Timor, India-Pakistan border, Bosnia and Herzegovina, Cyprus, Georgia, Croatia and Yugoslavia, Syrian Golan Heights, Iraq/Kuwait, Southern Lebanon, and the Middle East.

global defense spending. Such meager budgets cannot provide the types of equipment and training needed for projecting power well beyond state borders.

As a result, African states possess the ability to deploy and properly sustain no more than some 10,000 forces in aggregate. That figure assumes that those forces might need large numbers of vehicles or might have to operate in rural areas or other places where supplies could not be easily obtained from the indigenous economy. A number of African militaries can deploy considerably greater numbers of troops abroad if their forces carry only small arms and live off the civilian economies of the foreign countries in which they operate. That is generally plausible, however, only in cities that still have some rudiments of a functioning economy.[11]

Some 15,000 to 20,000 African troops have now received training and equipment for peace operations from the world's most modern militaries. In addition, more modest numbers of African military personnel have received general military education and training from programs such as the U.S. International Military Education and Training (IMET) and Joint Combined Exchange Training (JCET) programs.[12] The Africa

11. Roughly 100,000 foreign personnel have been involved in the current continuing conflict in Congo. The largest numbers from foreign armies were supplied by Rwanda, Uganda, and Zimbabwe; more than 50,000 *interahamwe*, the genocidal Hutu from Rwanda who were ultimately defeated in that country's 1994 civil war, are also believed to roam the country. Some of these forces operate within short distances of their home territories, but many do not. Of those far from home, many have been plundering the country. Thus these numbers have little to do with the kinds of capacities that would be needed to undertake humanitarian military missions.

12. The State Department–run International Military Education and Training program has an annual budget of $65 million and trains

Crisis Response Initiative (ACRI), recently renamed the African Contingency Operations and Training Assistance (ACOTA) program, was begun in 1997 by the Clinton administration to provide nonlethal and relatively simple assistance for permissive peacekeeping operations, generally those authorized under Chapter VI of the United Nations Charter, that are accepted voluntarily by warring parties. U.S. Special Forces and private American contractors together had trained nearly 9,000 troops, generally in battalion-sized units, by the end of 2001. The ultimate goal of the program has been to reach about 12,000 troops. Participating countries have included Senegal, Uganda, Malawi, Mali, Ghana, Benin, Côte d'Ivoire, and Kenya. Operation Focus Relief (OFR), the U.S. effort to provide lethal assistance to Nigeria, Senegal, and Ghana for a dangerous mission in Sierra Leone, reached roughly 4,000 troops during its period of intense activity in the late 1990s.[13] The ACRI was funded at

---

some 8,000 foreign military and civilian officials a year from a total of 125 countries. Averaging less than 100 students per country, it is clearly primarily designed to reach foreign elites rather than to prepare combat units—and its main purview is not peace operations, but much broader issues in defense policy, defense operations, and civil-military relations. See Department of State, *Foreign Military Training and DoD Engagement Activities of Interest, Volume I* (March 1, 2000), chapter 2, p. 2, available at www.state.gov/www/global/arms/fmtrain; U.S. Department of State, *Budget Tables, FY 2002 (2001)*, available at www.state.gov/s/rpp/rls/iab/index.cfm?docid=2104.

The Pentagon's Joint Combined Exchange Training (JCET) has an annual budget of about $15 million and involves training for U.S. as well as foreign forces in at least 110 countries. It also focuses on general military missions, and generally not on peace operations. See Dana Priest, "Free of Oversight, U.S. Military Trains Foreign Troops," *Washington Post*, July 12, 1998.

13. Douglas Farah, "Pentagon Role in Africa May End," *Washington Post*, July 3, 2001, p. A16; Ambassador Aubrey Hooks, "Pro-

roughly $20 million a year, though that amount has now been halved; OFR received funding of $20 million in total. Similar efforts undertaken by France under the RECAMP program (Reinforcement of African Peace-Keeping Capabilities) have added several thousand more troops to the total and are funded at roughly the level of ACOTA.[14] More modest efforts by Britain and several other countries have contributed as well.

Of those roughly 15,000 African troops who have been through one program or another, many have received only limited assistance. Training often lasts only ten to forty days; equipment generally includes only basics such as uniforms, eyeglasses, radios, night-vision goggles, water purification systems, and mine detectors. The United States tends to provide somewhat longer training, and France tends to provide a somewhat fuller suite of equipment, including some vehicles, but the overall rigor and comprehensiveness of each country's efforts are limited.

An expanded program is certainly feasible, as discussed further in chapter 4. A number of countries might be able to make smaller units available for training, even if they cannot marshal full battalions. In addition, some of the participating countries might be able to have a second or a third battalion trained, in addition to the first unit.[15] Finally, some countries that may

moting Security in Africa—the U.S. Contribution," paper presented at the Council on Foreign Relations, New York, N.Y., February 10, 2000, p. 4; Department of State, "The African Crisis Response Initiative," Fact Sheet, 2000; Daniel Benjamin, "The Limits of Peacekeeping," *Time Europe*, January 8, 2001.

14. Eric G. Berman and Katie E. Sams, *Peacekeeping in Africa: Capabilities and Culpabilities* (Geneva, Switzerland: United Nations Institute for Disarmament Research, 2000), pp. 267–376.

15. Ibid., pp. 288–89.

once have been considered ineligible for the program based on their human rights records or forms of government may deserve a second look.

The Bush administration's position on ACRI/ACOTA has been disappointing to date. It initially expressed an interest in expanding the effort, but, as noted, later reduced its budget request to $10 million for 2003.[16]

South and Southeast Asia

South Asian militaries have been at the core of UN peace-keeping missions for decades. Of these countries, India in particular has some power projection capability, as demonstrated by its wars against Pakistan and its interventions in the Maldives and Sri Lanka. The main South Asian nations continue to be among the largest contributors to UN missions today. Bangladesh leads all countries, with nearly 6,000 troops, and India and Pakistan together provide another 8,000 (see table 3-5). Thailand contributes nearly 500 troops to peace operations today; Malaysia has deployed about 2,000 at various times in recent years; Nepal and Indonesia have contributed several hundred troops to missions in the past as well.

Several South and Southeast Asian states have strong records of distinguished service in peacekeeping missions. Their troops are known for their professionalism and solid infantry soldiering skills. On average, they are perhaps not as excellent as most

16. Testimony by William M. Bellamy, Principal Deputy Assistant Secretary, Bureau of African Affairs, Department of State, before the House Committee on International Relations, Subcommittee on Africa, July 12, 2001.

Table 3-5. Top Contributors to UN Peacekeeping Operations as of June 30, 2002

Country	Observers	Police	Troops	Total
Bangladesh	65	131	5,254	5,450
Pakistan	76	343	4,398	4,817
Nigeria	56	75	3,320	3,451
India	37	606	2,379	3,022
Ghana	47	301	2,141	2,489
Kenya	55	57	1,747	1,859
Jordan	44	638	1,091	1,859
Uruguay	71		1,494	1,565
Ukraine	27	230	1,273	1,530
Australia	26	94	1,150	1,270

Source: Peace and Security Section of the Department of Public Information in cooperation with the Department of Peacekeeping Operations, United Nations. www.un.org/depts/dpko/dpko/contributors/june02.htm.

well-equipped and rigorously trained NATO soldiers, but they are generally competent, disciplined, and courageous.[17]

However, the armed forces of South and Southeast Asia are only modestly more capable than African militaries of deploying abroad quickly and sustaining themselves abroad independently. The fact that their units often include numerous reasonably well-trained and brave infantry soldiers does not mean that they have the integrated capacity to conduct power projection in hostile environments. In fact, given their generally limited defense budgets, the very fact of maintaining substantial numbers of proficient infantry soldiers makes it difficult also to provide them the necessary lift and logistics for operations abroad.

17. For one account of their performance in a difficult mission, see Mark Bowden, *Black Hawk Down* (Atlantic Press, 1999).

Latin America

Latin American countries have considerable military capabilities. Their aggregate defense budgets exceed those of sub-Saharan Africa and South and Southeast Asia combined. Brazil spends $17.5 billion a year on defense; Argentina and Mexico each spend about $5 billion; Chile, Colombia, and Venezuela each spend about $1.5 billion to $3 billion. Aggregate forces for all of Latin America, with 1.25 million troops, are not particularly large—but that can be a positive condition, since it means that more resources are available per individual soldier.

South American militaries have little capacity for power projection, however. Their political traditions do not tend to support such missions strongly, either. As is true of African militaries, most have focused on internal security rather than on war against neighbors or on overseas missions during their recent histories.

Nonetheless, South American countries have made contributions to peace and humanitarian missions. Argentina provided some 1,000 troops to UNPROFOR and has more than 600 peacekeepers in the field today. Uruguay is providing about 1,000 troops to peacekeeping missions at present. Others have contributed as well, though in smaller numbers. These forces are probably, on the whole, comparable to those of South and Southeast Asia in skill and equipment, but perhaps somewhat less experienced in and committed to peace operations.

China and Russia

Russian and Chinese forces are large enough so that, in theory, they could play significant roles in peace and humanitarian operations. In addition, some elements of each country's military are capable of operations in distant regions. However, both countries have been, and are likely to remain, focused on missions close to home. Moscow and Beijing also have political doubts about the desirability of humanitarian intervention as a matter of principle. For example, Russia's recent participation in Balkan operations probably reflects more of an interest in maintaining its influence in that part of the world than in peace and humanitarian missions per se.

Moreover, while both Russia and China have some power projection capabilities, each country's military also faces sharp physical constraints on its ability to deploy and sustain forces abroad. Despite China's having by far the largest military in the world, most of its units lack the transportation and logistics assets necessary to move far beyond the nation's borders. In fact, the Pentagon estimates that only about 20 percent of China's forces are capable even of moving about easily within PRC territory.[18] China has enough amphibious capacity to move 10,000 to 15,000 troops with medium-weight armor; its airborne capabilities may be sufficient to move about 6,000 more personnel, though few could deploy intercontinentally with their equipment, given the range limitations of the aircraft.[19] China's interest in keeping pressure on Taiwan and preoccupation with other nearby security concerns make it implausible that these forces can really be viewed as available

18. See William S. Cohen, "The Security Situation in the Taiwan Strait," Report to Congress pursuant to the FY99 Appropriations Bill (Washington, D.C.: Department of Defense, 1999), p. 11.

19. Ibid., p. 9; William S. Cohen, "Future Military Capabilities and Strategy of the People's Republic of China," Report to Congress pursuant to the FY98 National Defense Authorization Act (Washington, D.C.: Department of Defense, 1998), pp. 15–16.

for deployments—leaving aside the above-mentioned political constraints.

Russia's forces remain large and have impressive equipment inventories, at least on paper. However, that country's military has deteriorated badly in the past decade and become a largely hollow force, lacking adequate numbers of motivated and trained soldiers to fill its ranks and suffering from severe shortages in training, spare parts, and other necessities.[20]

The United States

The U.S. military has been reduced in size by roughly one-third since the cold war ended, with active-duty manpower declining from roughly 2.1 million to 1.4 million. The combat force structure of the U.S. military has also declined considerably over the past decade. Most types of units—such as Army divisions, Air Force wings, and the like—have been reduced by 20 percent to 40 percent.

Defense spending declined by about 20 percent, in real terms, over the course of the 1990s. But it is rebounding in the aftermath of the September 11 tragedy and is now scheduled to return to peak Reagan-era levels in real-dollar terms. The size of the military will remain at roughly 1.4 million active-duty troops, however, and force structure will remain at the lower levels noted above.

The U.S. military remains prepared for two nearly simultaneous major regional conflicts akin to Operation Desert Storm.

20. International Institute for Strategic Studies, *The Military Balance 2000/2001* (Oxford, England: Oxford University Press, 2000), pp. 109–10.

Secretary of Defense Donald Rumsfeld, in his September 30, 2001, quadrennial defense review, decided that only one of those wars should be assumed to be an all-out operation, possibly including the overthrow of an enemy regime and occupation of its territory. Nevertheless, the concept of two demanding, and geographically separate but chronologically overlapping, conflicts remains. The U.S. armed forces also retain responsibility for helping to defend the United States' friends and allies in Europe, the Middle East, East Asia, and Latin America. In fact, the number of these allies has increased since the cold war ended, as Poland, Hungary, and the Czech Republic have joined the NATO alliance, with more to follow. Overseas troop presence has been cut almost in half, from about 500,000 forces during the cold war to somewhat less than 300,000 today. By contrast with the cold war, however, today's overseas troops are more likely to be found on temporary deployments, not escorted by families and in remote locations. Roughly 100,000 U.S. military personnel are routinely found in East Asia, almost 120,000 in Europe, about 30,000 in the Persian Gulf region (as of mid-2002), and about 30,000 in and around Afghanistan. These overseas forces are intended to deter countries—including Iraq, North Korea, and China—from attacking their neighbors; to prevent friendly states from feeling the need to build undesirably large conventional forces or pursue nuclear weapons to ensure their security unilaterally; to give credibility to key alliances; and to promote American values.

Few Americans are generally involved in UN peace operations. At present, fewer than 1,000 participate, most of them police. But the United States does make substantial financial contributions to UN peacekeeping, averaging nearly $500 million annually over the past decade—despite its reluctance to pay its full dues during the late 1990s (see figure 3-1). It also has

Figure 3-1. U.S. Contributions to UN Peacekeeping, 1988–2002[a]

Millions of current-year dollars

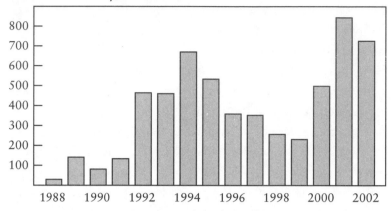

Source: Marjorie Ann Browne, "United Nations Peacekeeping: Issues for Congress," Congressional Research Service, updated April 18, 2001, pp. 10–11. Numbers for 2002 from Colin Powell's Testimony before the Senate Appropriations Committee, March 12, 2002.

a. The United States also provides money voluntarily through its Foreign Operations budget for non-UN peacekeeping operations, such as the African Crisis Response Initiative, efforts of the Organization for Security and Cooperation in Europe, and the Economic Community of West African States. The average voluntary contribution for the past five years has been $100 million a year.

typically spent about $2 billion a year in direct military costs for its own troops' participation in peace operations, most notably in Bosnia (see table 3-6).

As impressive as its capabilities and contributions are in size, it is in the area of global power projection that the U.S. military truly shines. Indeed, the ability of the United States to respond quickly to non-European crises abroad has improved considerably in the past decade. Fast sealift ships, known as roll-on/roll-off vessels, capable of operating in austere environments without sophisticated port infrastructure have been bought in considerable numbers. Total U.S. capabilities are adequate to carry the equivalent of at least three heavy ground divisions. Some of the ships are positioned overseas, with equipment already aboard, in places such as Guam, Diego Garcia in the Indian Ocean, and the Persian Gulf. The rest are in U.S. ports, ready to sail with little notice. Additional ships store equipment for the Marine Corps and the Air Force at those same overseas locations (the Marine ships provide another division's worth of prompt mobility). In addition, the Navy continues to have an amphibious fleet capable of transporting nearly a division of Marine forces. All told, on-call sealift could transport the equipment for four to five U.S. ground-combat heavy divisions at a time, and commercial aircraft that participate in a government program known as CRAF could quickly fly troops abroad to meet up with their equipment in a crisis.[21] Remarkably, total U.S. military sealift exceeds that of its major western allies combined by a factor of more than ten.

U.S. airlift capacities have not increased on balance, but they remain comparable to their cold war levels, and the airlift fleet is becoming more capable as C-17 planes replace older C-141s. If dedicated exclusively to transporting ground forces, the aggregate U.S. airlift fleet would theoretically be sufficient to transport almost all of a light infantry division at once. Aerial refueling capabilities are adequate to support these aircraft virtually anywhere in the world as well. Practical constraints, such as limited airfield capacity in overseas theaters, would probably reduce this throughput to no more than half the maximum theoretical potential. Even so, and even recognizing that some lighter divisions (notably the 101st Air Assault Division) weigh up to twice as much as a light infantry division,

21. See Rachel Schmidt, *Moving U.S. Forces: Options for Strategic Mobility* (Congressional Budget Office, 1997), pp. 23–44.

Table 3-6. Department of Defense Costs for Peace Operations, 1992–2002[a]

Budget authority in millions of current-year dollars through February 4, 2002

Country or region	Fiscal year											Total
	1992	1993	1994	1995	1996	1997	1998	1999	2000	2001	2002	
Bosnia	6	139	292	347	2,520	2,283	1,963	1,537	1,483	1,293	1,316	13,179
Kosovo								3,133	1,803	1,384	1,529	7,849
Air war								1,891				
KFOR								1,045	1,803	1,384		
Other[b]								197				
Haiti	9	3	372	569	87							1,040
Somalia	2	943	528	49								1,522
Rwanda		1	107	37								145
Angola	1	0.1	3									4
Cambodia	1	1	5									7
Western Sahara	1	0.3	0.1									1
East Timor								2	57	4		63
Totals												23,810

Source: Nina M. Serafino, "Peacekeeping: Issues of U.S. Military Involvement," Congressional Research Service, updated June 6, 2001 (data through 2/2002), pp. 15–16.

a. Totals rounded to the nearest million.

b. Includes prewar observer missions (Balkan Calm and Eagle Eye) and postwar refugee assistance (Sustain Hope).

most light forces could in theory be moved overseas within several weeks of a decision to do so.[22]

In addition to possessing impressive strategic transport capabilities, the United States fields military units that are inherently mobile and able to operate in austere environments overseas. Nearly all of its active ground forces, ten active Army divisions and three Marine divisions, could be operated abroad simultaneously and indefinitely—though they would need help from reservists for logistics support and other backup. These formations include more than 200,000 combat troops and twice as many support personnel.[23]

Putting together the pieces, the United States could transport at least two-thirds of its overall active-duty ground force capabilities, together with their associated logistics support, within three to four months of a decision to do so. In most situations actual deployments might be slower because Air Force assets and other equipment would compete with the Army and Marine Corps for airlift, and numerous airplanes would compete for refueling support.[24] Nonetheless, the theoretical capacity of the United States for rapid overseas deployment of ground force capabilities translates into the ability to move around 400,000 troops within ninety days.

22. Ibid., pp. 11–21.
23. See Frances Lussier, *Structuring the Active and Reserve Army for the 21st Century* (Congressional Budget Office, 1997), p. 11.
24. Ibid., pp. 15–20.

CHAPTER FOUR

AN AGENDA FOR IMPROVING INTERVENTION CAPACITY

Surveying the world's conflicts, both those now under way and those of the recent past, suggests that it would be desirable for the international community to have the capacity to deploy up to 200,000 troops at a time. Since some countries will choose not to participate in any given operation, and since troops will need to be rotated to avoid exhaustion and burnout, a total pool of perhaps 600,000 personnel would be desirable. That number is not exact; it is hard to know how troop rotations would work in advance. But a three-to-one ratio of available forces to deployed forces has generally been considered appropriate by the U.S. military. If anything, it is optimistic, and even more than 600,000 could be required to maintain 200,000 on deployment.[1]

1. In fact, on average the United States maintains no more than 10 percent of its forces on deployment, away from home station, at a time—somewhat more than 100,000 out of a total

As shown in table 3-1, the international community already has about that number of military personnel who can be rapidly deployed and then sustained in overseas theaters. The problem, however, is that two-thirds of the total number now come from the United States.

This fact may not be a major problem for traditional military missions. Even though greater burden sharing among major western allies would be desirable, the western alliance system appears to be achieving its main objectives of preserving stability, deterring conflict, and limiting the spread of weapons of mass destruction. However, as underscored in chapter 2, the situation is not nearly so good with regard to humanitarian intervention and muscular peace operations. Several missions that should have been undertaken have not been, often for the simple reasons that the United States is unwilling to provide most of the forces necessary and other countries cannot do enough. Nor is there any reason to think that Americans, who already shoulder a disproportionate share of the global military burden for handling traditional interstate conflict, should do far more than their share for humanitarian purposes. They should participate, but Americans should not have to be the world's policemen for civil conflicts. There is also no realistic chance that they will agree to play that role.

---

active-duty personnel strength of 1.4 million. Indeed, it considers that level of effort rather onerous. But that aggregate figure of 1.4 million includes many noncombat troops, so the ratio may be misleading. As another means of estimating availability, note that most U.S. military services have a policy of not letting individual personnel be absent from home for more than 120 days a year, essentially revalidating the 3:1 rule. See Michael O'Hanlon, *Defense Policy Choices for the Bush Administration,* 2d ed. (Brookings, 2002), pp. 28–62.

For these reasons, if there is to be additional effort in human-itarian and peace operations in the future, most forces are likely to come from other countries. That means that of the desired pool of 600,000 deployable military personnel, countries other than the United States should provide about 500,000 of the troops. In other words, those countries should more than dou-ble their aggregate power projection capabilities.

That number should be sobering for those who consider humanitarian military operations to require only relatively mod-est amounts of force. It should, however, be within reach for the international community, if not right away, then over time. To begin, not all troops need be equally well trained and equipped. Some missions will be less demanding than others. Some will not require rapid response or long-range transport. Either the peace accords that precede them will be negotiated over an extended period, allowing ample time for preparations, or the operations will be close to home for countries contributing troops. Even if 200,000 forces might be needed at a time, it is unlikely that it would be necessary to deploy more than 50,000 urgently. It is also unlikely that more than half to two-thirds would need to operate in extremely austere surroundings.

The Major Industrialized Democracies

Given their wealth, military proficiency, and commitment to human rights, other democracies have a crucial role to play in any global initiative to improve military capacity for humani-tarian intervention and for difficult peace operations.

Europe

If European countries are interested in playing a greater role on the world stage, they should take the step of increasing their military capabilities. That would enable them to become an important actor in traditional missions, such as Persian Gulf security. More important for the purposes of this study, it would also give them greater means to be major actors in humanitarian military intervention beyond their own continent. A number of European countries have contributed impressively to NATO's stability operations in the Balkans in recent years, and several have been important in smaller missions in Africa and, more recently, Afghanistan. However, their capacities for substantial, sustained, and rapid operations far from home territories are severely constrained.

The absence of a Soviet or Russian threat allows Europe's main powers to focus their military attentions beyond their own territories and continent and to fundamentally reassess the way they think of military power. NATO's European members field 2.4 million active-duty troops and another 3.7 million in the reserves (twice as many active forces, and more than three times as many reservists, as the United States). Even if Russia were still a threat, it wields a military force only a million strong— and its equivalent defense spending is less than $50 billion a year, in contrast to that of NATO Europe, which is $150 billion. For territorial defense, NATO member countries could easily make do with half as many troops and half as much defense spending as today.

Most European members of NATO as well as Canada should increase defense spending. Few of the major powers devote more than 2 percent of their gross domestic product to their militaries; even Britain and France devote no more than about 2.5 percent, in contrast to a U.S. level approaching 3.5 percent. Political realities and budgetary constraints being what they are, however, such desirable steps may prove infeasible. Even so, European countries in general could also develop adequate power projection capabilities without increasing their defense budgets if they cut forces further and used the resultant savings to purchase the necessary strategic transport and deployable logistics assets. Those that have not yet done so should also create all-volunteer units for deployment. These goals, central to the agenda at NATO's 2002 Prague summit, are already being promoted, so there is again some hope that this type of global agenda can succeed.

As argued in chapter 3, eight countries in north central and northwestern Europe have, for reasons of geography and available resources, the greatest latent military potential. These countries include Germany, France, the United Kingdom, Italy, Denmark, the Netherlands, Belgium, and Norway. With the exception of Britain and the partial exception of France, however, they have not yet exploited it.

A reasonable goal for these eight European members of NATO might be to further reduce the sizes of their armed forces, preserving their most modern equipment and units but otherwise scaling back to no more than 1.0 million total troops. That would essentially entail having the other European countries follow Britain's model of keeping a smaller, but better equipped and more professional, military. In addition, the major NATO European countries should purchase more strategic lift and more logistics equipment. Were this group of eight countries to organize its armed forces in the way Britain does today, it would be able to field 125,000 deployable troops on their own. Other EU countries could then make more modest contributions, together attaining the aggregate goal of 150,000 deployable soldiers and police set forth here.

Put in terms of major military units, this initiative might aim to develop eight to ten deployable and sustainable ground combat divisions. Breaking down the total country by country,

France, Germany, and the United Kingdom might each aim for two such divisions (a goal that Britain has already realized), Italy would aim for one to two, and the smaller key countries of northern Europe would each train and equip one or two brigades. The initiative would involve a comparable number of air wings. However, here the need for change would be less onerous because the weapons themselves are largely self-transportable and because the transport requirements for supplies are much less. Other NATO and EU members would ideally make modest contributions as well. This type of initiative would allow NATO allies to keep defense spending roughly at current levels, but would make Europe a serious second military pillar of the western alliance system (not only for humanitarian interventions and peacekeeping, but for war-fighting purposes as well, if desired).

The costs associated with making these ten divisions and wings deployable and self-sustainable are significant, but they are modest when placed in broader perspective: the $50 billion or so of investments that would be needed to make these forces deployable could easily triple the long-distance war-fighting and peacekeeping capabilities of countries that are already spending $150 billion each and every year on their defense establishments. A reasonable approach would be to devote $10 billion a year over five years for the necessary equipment and organizational changes. That would represent some 6 or 7 percent of total defense spending by the countries in question.

The Congressional Budget Office provided useful backup for these cost estimates in a 1996 study on the costs of NATO enlargement. The CBO estimated that roughly nine non-U.S. NATO ground divisions and ten air wings would require just over $15 billion in organic capabilities to be effective away from their home territories. That price tag, dominated by the ground force requirements, was for mobile hospitals, more trucks and heavy equipment transporters for tactical mobility, self-contained logistics like ammunition handling and storage units and equipment, more combat engineers and military police and mobile maintenance/repair units, and additional weapons capabilities such as artillery, air defenses, and transport helicopters. The CBO also identified two other major costs: aerial refueling tankers and stocks of fuel and munitions. The former, if scaled to represent roughly one-third of the overall U.S. capability, is about $10 billion; the latter is roughly the same, this time dominated by air wing requirements. Together with the costs for logistics, the running total is $35 billion.[2]

Additional costs for operating outside Europe would be necessary as well. They would be dominated by substantial amounts of strategic lift for troops, equipment, and fuel.[3] Assume that the eight NATO European countries mentioned above would, for reasons of economy, be content to possess one-third as much strategic airlift as the United States but would purchase one-half as much sealift as the U.S. armed forces (sealift being much cheaper than airlift).

For these purposes, one could view the cost of one hundred C-17 aircraft, or the equivalent, and roughly a dozen large roll-on/roll-off ships as a proxy. At roughly $300 million per airplane and $300 million per ship, that would translate into

2. Ivan Eland, "The Costs of Expanding the NATO Alliance," CBO Paper, Congressional Budget Office, March 1996, pp. 28–50.

3. See John E. Peters and Howard Deshong, *Out of Area or Out of Reach? European Military Support for Operations in Southwest Asia* (Santa Monica, Calif.: RAND Corporation, 1995), pp. 92–105.

about $35 billion in investment if procured as efficiently as the U.S. military could acquire such capabilities.[4] In that regard, reports that European countries are considering buying some two hundred A400M airlifters for roughly $80 million each are encouraging—though not yet sufficient, partly because their ranges are limited.[5]

Adding up the total costs makes for about $70 billion—but because some of these programs are already in the works, remaining investment requirements may be closer to $50 billion, as noted. Annual operating costs thereafter, dominated by the airlift fleet, would approach $750 million.[6]

Those programs already under way are not insignificant. Britain is planning to acquire two large roll-on/roll-off vessels. Under the defense plan of President Jacques Chirac, France plans to have at least 30,000 deployable troops and 100 deployable combat aircraft (roughly twice its Gulf War levels). France is also expanding its number of refueling aircraft from eleven to sixteen and envisioning an enhanced medium-range airlift fleet—as are a number of other European countries. Germany deployed thousands of combat forces to Bosnia and Kosovo in monumental decisions that were unprecedented since World War II; it also participated extensively in NATO's air war against Serbia in 1999. And in September 2002, NATO countries agreed to develop a 20,000-strong force for high-intensity

4. For a similar estimate calculated somewhat differently, see M. B. Berman and G. M. Carter, *The Independent European Force: Costs of Independence* (Santa Monica, Calif.: RAND Corporation, 1993), p. 24.

5. J. A. C. Lewis and Lale Sariibrahimoglu, "Europe Set to Repeat A400M Commitment," *Jane's Defence Weekly*, June 20, 2001, p. 3.

6. Rachel Schmidt, *Moving U.S. Forces: Options for Strategic Mobility* (Congressional Budget Office, February 1997), pp. 11, 62.

missions requiring quick response.[7] However, to date most European countries have made few efforts to acquire sealift, long-range airlift, and deployable logistics assets.[8]

Japan

More than half a century after World War II and more than a decade after the fall of the Berlin wall, Japan can and should do more in the international security sphere. It need not and should not mimic the United States, or even Great Britain. Unilateral power projection capabilities would unsettle some neighbors and displease many Japanese themselves. Nor need it even increase defense spending very much. Nevertheless, Japan should reexamine the basic way in which it structures and equips its military, a view with which Japan's leader, Prime Minister Junichiro Koizumi, has agreed.[9] It should also regain the momentum it began to establish in the early 1990s—when

7. See Bradley Graham and Robert G. Kaiser, "NATO Ministers Back U.S. Plan for Rapid Reaction Force," *Washington Post*, September 25, 2002, p. 24.

8. U.K. Ministry of Defence, *Defense White Paper 1996* (1996), paragraph 177; Stanley R. Sloan, "French Defense Policy: Gaullism Meets the Post–Cold War World," *Arms Control Today*, vol. 27, no. 2 (April 1997), pp. 6–7; interview with French Armed Forces Chief of Staff Gen. Jean-Philippe Douin, *Jane's Defence Weekly*, June 19, 1996, p. 112; Philip H. Gordon, "Does the WEU Have a Role?" *Washington Quarterly*, vol. 20, no. 1 (Winter 1997), p. 132; French Ministry of Defence, *1997–2015: A New Defence* (1997), pp. 26, 37, 57; and Jack Hoschouer, "NATO Mission Marks Germany's Military Policy Shift," *Defense News*, January 20–26, 1997.

9. National Institute for Research Advancement, *Japan's Proactive Peace and Security Strategies*, NIRA Research Report No. 20000005 (Tokyo, 2001), pp. 15–17.

it sent about seven hundred personnel to Cambodia in 1992–93 for peacekeeping and then four hundred to Zaire in 1994 for humanitarian relief after the Rwanda genocide—but has since largely lost, despite its deployment of support vessels and aircraft to the Indian Ocean to support the U.S. war in Afghanistan.[10]

In other Asian countries, many would oppose such a Japanese security policy out of fear of latent Japanese militarism. Within Japan, that worry exists too. But the alternative force structure outlined below would involve far too few troops to threaten countries such as China, Korea, the Philippines, or Vietnam. Yet the new capabilities would be quite substantial when measured against the demands of global humanitarian, peacekeeping, and peace enforcement missions.

Japan has many options besides becoming a "normal" power or remaining a civilian, largely pacifist power. A number of Japanese politicians, notably Ichiro Ozawa, have suggested what might happen.[11] The basic idea would be to expand the country's physical capacities for operations abroad, but keep legal, diplomatic, and military checks on these new capacities so as to reassure Japan's neighbors and the Japanese people about the nature of the effort. The goal would expressly *not* be for Japan to become an independent, global military power. Under such a framework, Japan would consider projecting power only in the context of multilateral security missions, preferably, if not exclusively, those approved by the UN

10. National Institute for Research Advancement, *Japan's Proactive Peace and Security Strategies*, p. 39.

11. See also Mike Mochizuki, ed., *Toward a True Alliance* (Brookings, 1997).

Security Council. It would not develop the physical capacity for doing more than that.

For encouragement, Japan and its neighbors might look to Germany. Not only has Germany sent combat forces to Bosnia and Kosovo for peace implementation, but it also recently dropped bombs on Serbia—a former World War II victim of Nazi aggression—in NATO's 1999 Operation Allied Force against Serbia. Germany also contributed forces to both the U.S.-led war effort in Afghanistan and the international security assistance force there. Granted, multilateral security structures comparable to NATO do not now exist in Asia, and Germany would not have acted as it did outside a NATO context. So the pace of change may wind up being slower in the case of Japan. Furthermore, the challenges are different. Nevertheless, change should still be possible.

If Japan chooses to move toward the proposed alternative national security policy and force posture, it will probably do so out of the recognition that its home islands are now much more secure against possible invasion than was the case during the cold war. That means that active-duty ground forces for territorial defense may not be needed in the numbers currently maintained. Reservists could be used in greater numbers for the territorial defense purpose if necessary, as in the cases of countries such as Switzerland and the Scandinavian nations. The Japanese army could reorient itself to become a smaller, more mobile organization, including an expeditionary ground capability of perhaps 25,000 individuals. That would allow sustained deployment of at least two brigades, as well as numerous other capabilities, such as military police and translators. Soldiers would be equipped for sustained operations abroad and trained for missions ranging from humanitarian relief to armed forcible intervention to quell civil conflicts, to hostage rescue and counterterrorism. The Japanese navy and air force could acquire the long-range transport assets needed to move the ground self-defense forces about.

These changes could be made without increasing Japan's roughly $40 billion annual level of defense expenditure. Japan's maritime self-defense forces would need to add only a modest amount of dedicated roll-on/roll-off sealift under this proposal. They might, for example, purchase enough to transport roughly one heavy division of ground forces—that is, their equipment and supplies for several weeks of operations. The United States has two categories of ships used most prominently for this purpose, SL-7s and large medium-speed roll-on/roll-off vessels (LMSRs); it presently owns about twenty in all (with a goal of twenty-seven). It takes about six to ten of these vessels to move a division and its supplies, depending on the precise nature of the division and the amount of support equipment and supplies transported. Thus Japan might buy ten. Alternatively, it could purchase smaller roll-on/roll-off ships, each with a capacity about one-third as great as the larger ships, that are more useful in small and shallow harbors and that have the added benefit of being less expensive (perhaps $40 million to $50 million versus $250 million to $300 million in cost per ship). Or, to gain the benefits of each type of ship, Japan might acquire a mix of perhaps four LMSR ships with a dozen smaller vessels. Total acquisition costs might be $1.5 billion to $2 billion, spread over roughly ten years. Modest annual operating costs of $50 million to $75 million would result thereafter.[12]

As for airlift and refueling aircraft, the United States is purchasing 120 C-17 aircraft; it also has 125 of the super-sized C-5s and operates about 160 C-141s as well, for a grand total

12. See Schmidt, *Moving U.S. Forces.*

of about 400 dedicated long-range transport planes. Under the above proposal for sealift, Japan would acquire roughly one-third of U.S. modern roll-on/roll-off capability and 10 to 20 percent of total U.S. military sealift by tonnage. Were it to seek a comparable amount of airlift, it would need to purchase thirty to sixty C-17s. For its refueling needs, Japan might purchase ten to twenty aircraft of roughly the size of the DC-10. It could also do what the United States does: purchase some planes usable for either refueling or transport (these are variants of the DC-10 known as KC-10s). All in all, Japan might purchase twenty C-17 lift aircraft and thirty KC-10 lift/refueling dual-purpose aircraft under this initiative. The cost of this initiative might be $250 million to $300 million per C-17 and about half that much per plane for the civilian aircraft. Total investment costs would approach $10 billion, with operating costs of $300 million to $500 million thereafter. Assuming a ten-year acquisition period, that translates to $1 billion a year in investment and would cost one-third to one-half as much thereafter. This would amount to less than 10 percent of the annual cost of the Japanese air forces.

The capacity of these assets would be significant but hardly threatening. A large military transport aircraft might hold 40 to 50 tons of equipment, meaning that Japan might be able to transport up to 2,000 tons per sortie using its entire fleet. However, a single heavy division in the U.S. military weighs about 100,000 tons, and even light and airborne or air mobile divisions weigh 20,000 to 30,000 tons apiece. In rough terms, the 2,000 tons of supplies that Japan could transport in a single trip would not be enough to equip more than 1,000 soldiers. This is a very modest capability. It could be significant for peace operations, particularly assuming secure airfields that permit rapid reinforcements with additional planeloads of supplies and people. It cannot be significant against a hostile foe with a sizable military, meaning that it should not excite real concern among Japan's neighbors.

New logistics support capabilities would also be needed. Notable on the list of required assets are mobile equipment repair depots and hospitals, transport trucks, mobile bridging and other engineering equipment, water purification and distribution systems, mobile fuel storage containers and dispensing equipment, and more mundane requirements such as food distribution and preparation facilities. In some types of peace operations, a number of these capabilities will not be needed, since host nations will be cooperative and ample time will be available to contract for indigenous logistics support. However, in more urgent, more hostile, or more rudimentary and undeveloped environments, one cannot assume that such capabilities will be present. About $5 billion might be needed for this hardware acquisition, using the cost factors assumed in the above analysis for NATO countries—averaging another $500 million a year over a decade-long period.

Developing Countries

Although their situations vary greatly from region to region and country to country, developing countries face many common budgetary challenges in any effort to expand military capabilities. Increased costs would follow from the need for more rigorous training and for better equipment.

Particularly in Africa, a continent facing numerous acute economic problems, the western powers will need to provide many of the resources required to expand and improve regional military capabilities. Programs now under way, such as the U.S. Africa Crisis Response Initiative (ACRI), recently renamed the

African Contingency Operations and Training Assistance (ACOTA) program, as noted earlier, are important steps in the right direction. But they do not involve nearly enough troops or provide sufficiently rigorous training and sufficiently capable equipment.

The need for more rigorous training is evident. Under current assistance programs, exercises and classes typically take no more than a few weeks. Yet creating a highly ready military, competent across a broad spectrum of operations, including combat, typically takes many months if not longer.[13] As a U.S. Army field manual puts it, "The most important training for peace operations remains training for essential combat and basic soldier skills"—underscoring the scope of the challenge for preparing good troops for such missions.[14] In addition, troops conducting peace and humanitarian interventions also must work with nongovernmental organizations that provide relief and other services, adding further complexities to any mission.[15] The United States and other foreign militaries cannot be expected to build other countries' armed forces up from the ground level; nor would any such offers necessarily be well received. But months of training, as opposed to weeks, are needed. So are refresher courses every one to two years. At least

13. For a good explanation of how hard the U.S. military needed to work to improve its own standards after Vietnam, see Robert H. Scales Jr., *Certain Victory: The U.S. Army in the Gulf War* (Washington, D.C.: Brassey's, 1994), pp. 1–38.

14. U.S. Army, *Field Manual 100-23: Peace Operations* (Washington, D.C., 1994), available at www.adtdl.army.mil/cgi-bin/atdl.dll/fm/100-23/fm100-23.htm, chapter 3, p. 8.

15. See, for example, Chris Seiple, *The U.S. Military/NGO Relationship in Humanitarian Interventions* (Carlisle Barracks, Pa.: U.S. Army War College Peacekeeping Institute, 1996); Daniel Byman and

a doubling in the intensity of training per unit is appropriate. Exercises are also needed to practice coordinating operations at higher and larger levels of effort—notably, for missions involving brigades and divisions. Most of these exercises can be headquarters and staff efforts, as opposed to full-scale field training, but they are critical.

To get a handle on the costs of serviceable equipment for such countries, two different approaches can be taken. One is to examine the costs of a country that has typically tried, successfully, to field strong ground forces with fairly low defense spending, such as Turkey ot South Korea. This approach tends to produce cost estimates that are somewhat too low, perhaps, since such countries do not typically buy large amounts of strategic lift or deployable logistics support equipment.

Another way is to examine the U.S. Marine Corps budget. Since the Marines are very sustainable abroad, their budget does cover the costs of deployable logistics (though not the costs of strategic transport, which are provided for them by the Air Force and especially the Navy). Cost estimates produced in that way may wind up high, however, given the more costly equipment usually purchased by even the most frugal of the U.S. military services. But it explicitly accounts for support forces of various types—medical crews, engineering and construction companies, firefighting units, communications specialists, and so forth—that are just as critical in many operations as infantry soldiers themselves. An international effort to improve African capacities should aspire to attain levels as close

---

others, *Strengthening the Partnership: Improving Military Coordination with Relief Agencies and Allies in Humanitarian Operations* (Santa Monica, Calif.: RAND Corporation, 2000).

to those of the Marine Corps as possible, given the desirability of possessing organic logistics support capabilities and combat capabilities in regions far removed from the domestic infrastructure of the countries sending forces. Useful benefits can be attained at lower levels of effort as well, however.

South Korea has, over the past couple of decades, averaged expenditure of some $10 billion to $12 billion on its military, with about $3 billion to $4 billion typically going to procurement.[16] With that budget, it fields half a million active-duty ground forces, most of them light infantry, but with substantial numbers of armored and mechanized formations as well. In other words, the types of units in South Korea's military are probably a good model for what one would want to create in the way of global intervention capacity. South Korea's equipment inventories have been built up over two to three decades. Given the normal lifetimes of most weaponry, and since a good deal of South Korea's procurement budget has gone to its air force and navy, its ground forces probably field about $50 billion in equipment. Since those forces comprise 450,000 troops, the value of their equipment is roughly $10 billion per 100,000 soldiers.

The U.S. Marine Corps, over the past twenty years, has typically spent $1.5 billion to $2 billion procuring ground-combat equipment for nearly 200,000 Marines. It has thus acquired $30 billion to $35 billion in equipment for 150,000 Marines focused on ground combat. These numbers suggest a cost of about $20 billion per 100,000 ground troops.

16. See various issues of the International Institute for Strategic Studies' *Military Balance* (current issues are published by Oxford University Press), as well as South Korea, Ministry of National Defense, *Defense White Paper 1997–1998* (Seoul, 1998), pp. 136, 190.

Suppose that the world's developing countries chose to field well-equipped deployable ground forces, including 100,000 soldiers, as well as comparable numbers of well-trained soldiers with somewhat less equipment and more limited capabilities. The cost for the first 100,000 soldiers might then be $10 billion to $20 billion, and the cost of the second group perhaps half as much. If the purchases were not done in a coordinated manner, unit costs might go up somewhat, as would subsequent maintenance costs. At the same time, if second-hand equipment were sometimes acquired, costs could be less.

Poor countries, principally in Africa, might receive such equipment as aid. The donor community might spend up to $20 billion to make such an arrangement work. The U.S. share might be $7 billion to $8 billion, assuming that Europe would provide an equal amount and that countries such as Japan would contribute significant assistance as well. If provided during a ten-year initiative, annual U.S. aid would be about $750 million for this purpose; operating and training costs could drive the total close to $1 billion. Including support from all donors, annual costs would total $2 billion to $3 billion a year.

The proposed U.S. assistance figure is dozens of times higher than past spending for the Africa Crisis Response Initiative and Operation Focus Relief combined, and comparable to the entire U.S. assistance budget for Africa. However, it is several times less than current U.S. military aid to the Middle East. Total assistance from all donors under this proposal would be several times less than what Africans themselves spend on their armed forces (about $10 billion a year) and almost ten times less than total economic aid to Africa (about $20 billion a year). Moreover, such levels need not be attained overnight, if at all, since scaled-back programs could be useful as well. This calculation is an estimate of what it would cost to create an idealized intervention and peacekeeping capability for the international community. Much more modest, and politically realistic, efforts would themselves be highly useful.

Costs might also be reduced if central UN equipment stockpiles, such as those now in place in Brindisi, Italy, were expanded. In that case, national militaries would not need as much equipment for themselves, and stockpiles could be sized to the expected scale of deployments rather than to the need for a large rotation base as well. This approach is worthy of consideration, especially if transport assets can be earmarked in advance for use in taking the equipment to where it might need to be used.[17] But it would probably be better, for the sake of training, to provide at least some capacities directly to national militaries.

Substantial numbers of U.S. personnel might be needed to carry out the associated training. For example, 150 special forces personnel were involved in Operation Focus Relief in 2001 for a program training just 4,000 troops.[18] Were that program increased by a factor of ten, more than 1,000 special forces troops might be needed, out of a total of only 30,000 active-duty special forces in the U.S. inventory. However, such a large number of special forces could not realistically be provided, so private contractors such as MPRI would probably have to be hired, adding several tens of millions of dollars to the required annual budget. Such an additional expense is well worth it given the severity of the problem of civil violence in the world today.

17. Lakhdar Brahimi and others, *Report of the Panel on United Nations Peace Operations* (New York: United Nations, 2000), p. 14.
18. Segun Adeyemi, "Special Forces Teach Peace Support Skills," *Jane's Defence Weekly*, May 23, 2001.

If programs such as ACRI/ACOTA and Operation Focus Relief are expanded to more countries and used more systematically to provide combat-related or lethal aid to militaries, some problems will result. Notably, abuses will occur, and soldiers who have been trained by the United States will sometimes commit them. Individual acts of violence would be likely; atrocities like those that made the U.S. School of the Americas for Latin American soldiers so controversial could not be ruled out entirely.[19] In a truly extreme case, a country that the United States has chosen as a security partner may dissolve into conflict or coup.[20] Indeed, ACRI training in Côte d'Ivoire was suspended following its recent coup. As another concern, countries trained and equipped by the United States could even wind up fighting each other.

Every step must be taken to minimize the chances of such unwanted consequences, but in the end they cannot be completely prevented—and the United States should be braced accordingly. Provided that proper precautions are observed, careful personnel screening processes used, and sound training programs implemented, the international community should accept the associated risks, particularly in Africa, where conflict is so widespread and so deadly. The alternative to training and equipping soldiers is often unchecked war, in which thousands

19. For one powerful critique of the School of the Americas, see Roy Bourgeois, "Army School's New Name Won't Disguise Atrocities," *Atlanta Journal and Constitution*, January 28, 2001.

20. Such risks exist even in important and promising countries such as Nigeria and South Africa; see Gwendolyn Mikell and Princeton N. Lyman, "Critical U.S. Bilateral Relations in Africa: Nigeria and South Africa," Center for Strategic and International Studies, Washington, D.C., April 2001.

and tens of thousands will die, or even genocide. Seen against this backdrop, inaction is usually the worse risk, and developing greater capacity among developing countries for humanitarian action is the most sound and moral course.

The United States

The United States needs to continue to play a role in responding to humanitarian emergencies. The reality is that other countries do not in general have the forcible entry capabilities or sustainable logistics to intervene in distant lands to save lives, nor are most of them likely to obtain such capabilities quickly. That is, they do not have the long-range airlift and sealift, the mobile hospitals and equipment repair facilities, the equipment to develop airfields in austere locations if necessary, and the large quantities of trucks and engineering equipment to operate at great distance from modern infrastructure for extended periods.[21] Over time, this fact can and should change, as this book argues. To date it has not, nor will it likely change dramatically in the next five years or so. As much as the United States should encourage, and in some cases even aid, the evolution of other countries' power projection capabilities, as discussed above, it also needs to assume that in some cases it will continue to carry out—or at least initiate—such missions with limited help from other countries.

21. See, for example, Richard Sokolsky, Stuart Johnson, and F. Stephen Larrabee, eds., *Persian Gulf Security: Improving Allied Military Contributions* (Santa Monica, Calif.: RAND Corporation, 2000), especially p. 83; Peters and Deshong, *Out of Area or Out of Reach?* pp. 77–120; and Ivan Eland, "The Costs of Expanding the NATO Alliance" (Washington, D.C.: Congressional Budget Office, 1996), pp. 28–50.

Moreover, the United States stands to benefit diplomatically and otherwise by doing its share. Contributing to peace and humanitarian missions underscores to the international community that the United States has broader security interests beyond ensuring its own stability, safety, and prosperity. It thus helps maintain the moral legitimacy of U.S. leadership and gives at least some countries outside the western alliance network reasons to think that they too benefit from America's role in the world. These benefits may be intangible, but they are not negligible or unimportant.

Even if the international community does not conduct more interventions in the future than it has in the past, simply maintaining the same level of effort will require adjustments in the U.S. military. The past twelve years have been hard on a force built first and foremost for major war, but in practice also asked to feed Kurds in Iraq, help make and then keep the peace in Bosnia and Kosovo, relieve starvation in a hostile environment in Somalia, take care of refugees from Rwanda in Zaire, and push corrupt governments out of power in Panama and Haiti and Afghanistan.

Some have suggested creating new types of formations dedicated to handling these missions. The logic for this proposal is either that humanitarian interventions and peace operations are so different from combat as to require a different basic type of expertise, or that combat units conducting such secondary missions lose their warrior spirit and combat edge.

In fact, both arguments are weak. This is probably good news for proponents of humanitarian intervention, since creating dedicated units that would perform only one type of mission or the other would drive defense budget costs up substantially. In today's military, a single type of unit can and does undertake both combat and peace operations, as circumstances require. Since the U.S. combat forces are sized conservatively, based on a so-called two-war strategy, there are generally combat forces available to conduct a secondary mission—provided that such missions are not conducted so frequently as to "break the force" by excessively taxing people and equipment.[22]

The suggestion that U.S. combat forces are incapable of conducting peace operations well is belied by their admirable track record. Incidents of soldiers overreacting to provocations from unruly mobs or otherwise using too firm a hand in situations better handled quietly have been few and far between. Missions in places like Somalia, Haiti, and Bosnia that succeeded in some ways but fell short in others never failed due to the poor performance of troops on the ground. In Somalia, political and military leadership made mistakes, but U.S. soldiers still fought well in the infamous October 3, 1993, firefight. In Haiti, it has proven very difficult to reform national institutions and create a more constructive political environment—but these are not tasks that U.S. troops would have been expected to carry out in any case. In Bosnia, the fact that the three ethnic entities have not reintegrated themselves is explained by the realities of the local politics, not by the weakness of NATO's patrols or other deficiencies in its soldiers' performance. Perhaps the international community needed to do a better job in these places. Perhaps a stronger and more vigorous effort was required at the level of policing, purging corrupt and dangerous individuals

22. Even though he is a skeptic of many peace operations, Secretary of Defense Donald Rumsfeld has actually made it somewhat easier to countenance smaller missions like humanitarian interventions by adopting a somewhat less demanding and constricting form of two-war strategy. See Secretary of Defense Donald H. Rumsfeld, *Quadrennial Defense Review Report* (Washington, D.C.: Department of Defense, 2001).

from politics, and strengthening legal institutions. More robust rules of engagement for military forces might have contributed to a more favorable outcome as well. But NATO and U.S. troops were perfectly capable of establishing and maintaining security as requested and of doing so without inflaming tensions through ill-considered uses of force.

Not only do soldiers seem capable of being peacekeepers, but sometimes their soldiering skills come in handy as well. Many countries around the world—several South Asian and Southeast Asian states, many smaller European countries, and others—are capable of providing competent soldiers skilled in basic patrolling and small-arms use for traditional peacekeeping missions where the threat of renewed violence is low. These are not missions in which U.S. combat forces need generally participate, unless there is a pressing political reason that they do so. American forces are needed precisely where combat is possible—such as in Somalia, or Haiti, or Bosnia. In cases where they do not wind up fighting, their reputations as formidable warriors undoubtedly help to explain that outcome. This intimidation factor is desirable, and not one that should be sacrificed lightly. Even in cases where local militias are not inclined to challenge outside forces, many of the operations involved in establishing control of a country—taking airfields, protecting relief convoys, protecting against possible ambushes, flying helicopters around a potential combat zone—require the skills of soldiers.

As for the second allegation—that warriors should not be charged with peace operations because they weaken their fighting spirit and detract from their training regimens—the concern is real, but the evidence supporting it is generally weak. First of all, many soldiers like the work of peace operations, as evidenced by the relatively high reenlistment rates of soldiers who have deployed to the Balkans. Second, they can train at the small-unit level even while deployed. Third, restoring their large-unit maneuver and combat skills admittedly takes a while—from three to six months, depending on which estimate one accepts. However, if only 5 to 10 percent of the combat force structure is involved in carrying out a peace operation or recovering from one at any time, that burden is entirely manageable. Indeed, there is not enough strategic lift in the U.S. military to carry all forces to a combat theater in less than four to six months in any case. Thus, in the event of a major conflict (or two), units that have recently been engaged in peace operations can train while others deploy first.[23]

It is true that humanitarian and peace operations have put additional strain on a military that is not particularly large and that is already heavily employed. But that is partly due to the way in which the military was organized and used—as well as to missions in Iraq and Northeast Asia and other traditional deployments, which remained the most demanding on the military.[24] For example, the Army overused the 10th Mountain

23. See Statement of Army General George Joulwan before the House National Security Committee, March 19, 1997, pp. 12–14; Statement of Mark E. Gebicke, General Accounting Office, before the House National Security Committee's Subcommittee on Readiness, March 11, 1997, pp. 3–4; Thomas F. Lippiatt and others, *Post-mobilization Training Resource Requirements: Army National Guard Heavy Enhanced Brigades* (Santa Monica, Calif.: RAND Corporation, 1996), pp. xv–xviii, 1–21; Schmidt, *Moving U.S. Forces*, p. 79; and Frances Lussier, *Structuring the Active and Reserve Army for the 21st Century* (Washington, D.C.: Congressional Budget Office, 1997), pp. 7–11.

24. For an overview of the state of U.S. military readiness in 2000, see O'Hanlon, *Defense Policy Choices for the Bush Administration*, pp. 28–62.

Division in the early 1990s in Somalia and Haiti, putting most burdens for intervention on its shoulders simply because it wanted to keep other units free for a possible two-war scenario. The Army also routinely kept units under strength during most of the 1990s, meaning that it would have to bring a deploying unit up to full manpower by raiding other units. That practice, also attributable to the two-war construct that mandated keeping ten large active Army divisions, and a large support base, created a ripple effect through the force that caused far greater strain than modest-sized deployments should have.

Secretary Rumsfeld fixed part of this problem by changing the two-war demands on the military. No longer envisioning two simultaneous conflicts like Desert Storm, the Pentagon now envisions one such all-out war, possibly including the overthrow of an enemy leader and occupation of that country's territory, together with a second, smaller operation elsewhere. By keeping the same force structure for a less demanding two-war requirement, Rumsfeld should have eased the military's ability to prepare for and conduct other missions.

That said, more concrete changes are needed as well. Certain types of units should be augmented in number. These include special forces with particular language and political skills, military police, and support units that provide water and food and medical care, not only to troops but also to indigenous civilian populations in many humanitarian missions. Some of these units, many of which are found primarily in the reserve force structure since they do not require constant training and drilling to do their jobs in war, are being overused. It would be desirable to place more of them in the active-duty force structure so that they can be deployed without causing excessive disruption to the lives of reservists who did not expect such duty short of a major national crisis.

For example, Army data show that 12,000 more personnel would be needed to relieve excessive burdens on existing "high demand/low density" units, such as those making up military police units. Corresponding annual costs for the Army would not exceed $1 billion.[25]

Conclusion

The international security environment, while generally stable among the great powers, is not nearly so good in regard to civil warfare and internal conflict. This may be a secondary element of the broader international system, given that most such wars are in poor and distant lands and that few mutate into more serious interstate conflicts. Nonetheless, it is an important element of the international order. Those who have insisted that such warfare would inevitably worsen with the end of the cold war and the continued growth in global populations have not had their worst fears realized to date. Unfortunately, they could still be proved right. More to the point, the violence remains serious, even if it has not intensified appreciably in the recent past, and the associated toll in lives destroyed remains extremely tragic. And failed states can contribute, at least indirectly, to the success of global terrorist networks, which can use such states as sanctuaries, for acquiring resources, and in some cases for finding willing recruits.[26]

25. See General Accounting Office, *Contingency Operations: Providing Critical Capabilities Poses Challenges*, GAO/NSIAD-00-164 (July 2000); and Laurinda Zeman, *Making Peace While Staying Ready for War: The Challenges of U.S. Military Participation in Peace Operations* (Washington, D.C.: Congressional Budget Office, 1999), p. xix.

26. Robert I. Rotberg, "Failed States in a World of Terror," *Foreign Affairs*, vol. 81, no. 4 (July/August 2002), pp. 127–41.

IMPROVING INTERVENTION CAPACITY

The United States cannot be indifferent to such realities for they help shape the broad character of the global environment and thus the way in which American leadership is assessed and perceived by the rest of the world. Other industrialized democracies, with their equal commitments to human rights, cannot be indifferent either—and cannot expect the United States to carry this military burden too, just as it carries the primary military burden for defending their access to oil, limiting the dangers from proliferation, and generally helping to preserve peace among the great powers. Developing countries are the ones whose peoples generally suffer in civil conflict and whose territories are often inundated with refugees or armed militias when wars happen in their neighborhoods, so they cannot be indifferent either.

The world community has attempted to quell the worst effects of civil conflict in recent years, but its efforts have fallen short. There are many reasons; wars are simply difficult to stop even when one has the tools to stop them. They require a good deal of time and attention from top officials in key countries and organizations—to understand the local actors at work in a given conflict, to devise workable military interventions, to orchestrate the international coalition-building needed to legitimate an intervention and create a multilateral military force to carry it out, and then to follow up the military instrument with effective efforts at economic and political recovery.

In some cases, the main explanation for the international community's shortcomings is that it does not have enough of the requisite military and police forces to carry out such missions promptly and effectively. As a result, some interventions are handled well, whereas others are not considered or are attempted on the cheap. The contrast is telling between tens of thousands of NATO-led troops keeping the peace in small

Bosnia and tiny Kosovo, on the one hand, and the decision to use just 3,000 UN personnel to monitor a possible peace in the Democratic Republic of Congo—with ten times the population and forty times the land area of Bosnia and Kosovo combined—on the other.

It will take time to change this situation, to be sure. However, serious efforts from several of the world's major regions and countries can make the broader problem solvable. Major western countries need not greatly increase defense spending, but they do need to change their defense priorities—and Washington needs to support their efforts to do so, rather than fear a weakening of its alliances simply because its advanced allies seek somewhat greater military autonomy. Developing countries need to train and equip their forces better. A serious and sustained effort is required, and international assistance is essential. The scale of the American contribution need not be especially onerous—resources on the order of $1 billion a year and quite modest numbers of uniformed military personnel to act as trainers would be sufficient. Proportionate efforts would be needed from other major industrial democracies as well.

The rough outlines of a greater global capacity for humanitarian intervention and peace operations might be as follows. Countries would not need to add troops to their armed forces in general. In fact, they would generally be better advised to reduce overall troop numbers to free up funds that could be used to improve the capacities of their remaining units for rapid deployment and sustainable operations abroad.

The United States would make modest improvements in parts of its force structure to facilitate the types of deployments it has carried out over the past decade and to make possible a slightly greater level of effort in the future. European Union nations would more than double their Headline Goals for rapid force deployment from the stated 60,000 to 150,000 troops, committing to buy the sealift, airlift, and logistics needed to make those numbers meaningful. These forces could clearly also be useful for other missions, such as defeating aggression in the Persian Gulf, if the EU countries so desired.

Japan might aim only half as high as a large European country in terms of the number of troops it had available for deployment. It would also purchase strategic lift to transport its own self-defense forces as well as other militaries. Countries such as Canada and New Zealand would make at least modest improvements in their capabilities as well. Australia might do likewise, though it has less need for improvement.

African countries, with financial help and training assistance from the United States and western Europe and Japan, would seek to develop the capacity for deploying at least 50,000 fully equipped troops abroad. It would also seek the capacity for deploying another 50,000 personnel, proficient in infantry skills and peace operations, even if they were not fully outfitted for autonomous military operations in austere environments. South and Southeast Asia would collectively adopt comparable goals. South American states would be somewhat less ambitious, but would pursue an aggregate capacity of close to 50,000 deployable and sustainable troops.

However, not all countries will be capable of major, near-term improvements in capacity. Nations such as Turkey and South Korea are unlikely to be able to play a greater role in the near term given more immediate security concerns. Russia and China should do more, and they should be prodded to do more. However, they are unlikely to be willing or able to contribute large numbers of proficient forces, given their ideological reservations about such military activities, their own more immediate security concerns, and their military limitations.

Taken together, achieving these goals would provide some 500,000 non-American troops for humanitarian and peace operations, together with adequate lift and logistics for rapid and sustained operations. They would give the international community the resources it needs to make a serious and fairly systematic effort at reducing the human tolls associated with the world's most violent wars.

The roughness of these numbers needs to be constantly emphasized. First, the basic notion that 200,000 troops might have to be deployed in global humanitarian missions at any given time is highly approximate, based on assuming that the future will resemble the recent past or the present. That assumption could easily prove wrong.

Second, not all troops need be exactly equal in capabilities. Some will be backed up by strong logistics capabilities and capable of difficult operations in remote regions; others will depend largely on the infrastructure of the countries to which they deploy for food, fuel, water, housing, medical care, and/or equipment maintenance. In some missions, the latter forces will not be up to the task. The goal of the agenda developed here is to create pools of forces that possess organic logistics support permitting them to operate independently far from cities and in the face of hostile resistance, but that goal will not be achieved by all forces.

Third, forces that are equipped and trained for peace operations or humanitarian interventions may be used for other purposes too. European military forces improved largely with humanitarian goals in mind may be used for heavy combat in the Persian Gulf, for example; African or South Asian military forces may be used for domestic counterinsurgency missions or other purposes. Creating a larger pool of deployable forces thus does not guarantee that they will always be made available for the intended purposes. That is part of the reason why it is necessary to create a larger pool of additional forces than one would ever expect to see deployed simultaneously.

More desirably, the fact that forces usable for humanitarian or peace operations could be used for other purposes may increase the incentives of countries to support this type of agenda. They can gain domestic benefits even as they also contribute to a worthy international goal.

Nearly half a million persons, most of them civilians and many of them children, continue to die each year because of the immediate effects of war. Most of the deaths typically take place in just a few countries at a time, meaning that it is not an intractable proposition to do something about it. The international community must find the means to reduce that tragic human toll. Doing so is well within its reach politically as well as financially. However, a global plan of action and a coordinated global effort are required.

INDEX

INDEX

Humanitarian intervention;
Military troops; Peacekeeping
operations
Clinton, Bill, 19, 20
Colombia: civil conflict in, 3;
projectable military forces, 76
Combined Joint Task Force
(CJTF), 60, 61
Conflict resolution, critique of
literature, 7
Congo: civil conflict, 3, 14, 33, 48;
peacekeeping operation in, 34t,
41–42, 67, 113; size of forces
needed for stability, 43
Côte d'Ivoire, training programs
for troops, 72, 104
Croatia, peacekeeping operation
in, 34t
Cyprus, peacekeeping mission in,
5, 34t
Czech Republic as NATO member,
79

Dallaire, Romeo, 8
Defense as military focus: European countries, 59; Latin
America, 76
Defense budgets: Africa, 67,
100–01; Australia, 63; Canada,
63; change in priorities, 113;
Japan, 65, 96, 98; Latin
America, 76; NATO Europe,
55, 56t, 88; New Zealand, 63;
Russia, 88; South Korea,
63–64; Turkey, 63–64; U.S., 51,
56t, 78

Denmark: in Gulf War, 60; projectable military forces, 55, 56t,
89
Developing countries: defense
budgets, 100–01; equipment
needs, 100, 102; improving
intervention capacity, 98–105;
need to address civil conflicts,
112; projection of military
forces, 66–67; training for,
99–100, 113. See also Africa;
individual countries
Draft, 58, 61
Drug war, 20
Duration of interventions, 44

East Timor: Australian involvement, 63; humanitarian
intervention in, 5, 35; UN
peacekeeping operation, 34t
Economic aid, 16, 102
Egypt, in peacekeeping missions,
67
El Salvador, humanitarian
intervention in, 5
Eritrea/Ethiopia, peacekeeping
operation in, 34t, 67
Ethiopia, in peacekeeping
missions, 67
Eurocorps, 60
Europe: civil conflict in, 2; in Gulf
War, 60; improving intervention
capacity, 87–93, 113; projectable forces, 55–63, 88; transport
needs, 59, 61, 62t, 90–93. See
also NATO; individual countries

Venezuela, projectable military
forces, 76
Volunteer units, 89

Western Sahara, peacekeeping
operation in, 34t, 67. *See also*
individual countries

Yugoslavia, peacekeeping
operation in, 34t

Zaire. *See* Rwanda
Zambia, in peacekeeping missions,
66